# Smile

## How do you stop the memories from fading?

Ian Loftus

OTHER MINDS
PUBLISHING

Copyright © IP Loftus 2023

The right of IP Loftus to be identified as the author of this work has been asserted by him in accordance with the Copyright, Designs and Patents Act 1988.

All rights reserved. No part of this publication may be reproduced, stored in or introduced into a retrieval system or transmitted, in any form, or by any means (electronic, mechanical, photocopying, recording or otherwise) without prior permission of the publisher. Any person who does any unauthorised act in relation to this publication may be liable to criminal prosecution and civil claims for damages.

For more information, contact:
connect@ianploftus.com
https://ianploftus.com

Book design by RJ Loftus MA
Cover design by RJ Loftus MA

ISBN – Paper back: 9798863303871
First Edition: October 2023

**This book is dedicated to Dominic 'Dom' Loftus
16 January 1991–4 October 2013**

*'Susan was already three months pregnant when she told me.
I went for a long walk down a Cumbrian country lane.
After a while, the sky seemed bluer, and the grass was much greener.
All lives begin before the first breath is even taken.
Some lives continue long after the last breath has been drawn.'*
IP Loftus

**In Memory of Lucy Dec 2011 – July 2023**

# CONTENTS

SMILER ............................................................................................. I

CONTENTS ...................................................................................... V

FOREWORD ................................................................................... IX

PART 1 - LOSS AND AVOIDANCE ............................................. XIV

DIDN'T YOU USED TO BE IAN LOFTUS? ...................................... 1

NARROW FIELD OF VISION ........................................................... 8

THE GOOD OLD DAYS ................................................................. 16

    9TH OCTOBER 2013 ................................................................. 18

    11TH OCTOBER 2013 ............................................................... 19

    14TH OCTOBER 2013 – THE WESTMORLAND HERALD ............ 19

        *Lost keys* ............................................................................. 22

18 OCTOBER 2013 – ST ANDREW'S CHURCH – PENRITH ........ 23

A SMALL STEP .............................................................................. 26

'NO ONE EVER TOLD ME THAT GRIEF FELT SO MUCH LIKE FEAR' ......... 28

    FADE TO BLACK ....................................................................... 28

    FADE TO WHITE ...................................................................... 29

    SORROW ................................................................................. 29

    REGRET .................................................................................. 29

    3 OCTOBER 2014 .................................................................... 30

    4 OCTOBER 2014 .................................................................... 30

    A KIND OF KINDRED SPIRIT... .................................................. 33

EARLY INFLUENCES – GODS, CAESAR AND MUNGO .............. 40

    28 JULY 2014, 10.38 AM .......................................................... 44

**SEVENTEEN** ............................................................................................... **47**
    *7 December 2013, at 14:57 (email)* ....................................................... 54
    *10 December 2013* ................................................................................. 55
    *15 January 2014, The Letter from Dominic* ......................................... 55
    TODAY IS THE DAY OF DOMINIC'S BIRTH, 16TH JANUARY 1991 ......................... 57

**HELEN** ...................................................................................................... **58**
    *23 February 2014, 2.30 pm, Eden Valley Hospice*............................... 59

**THE LETTER TO SUSAN** ........................................................................... **61**

**A DISPLACEMENT ACTIVITY** .................................................................... **63**

**A FAUSTIAN DEAL** .................................................................................. **65**

**5 NOVEMBER 2014** ................................................................................. **67**

**TO SMILE, OR NOT TO SMILE?** ............................................................... **72**

**DOM'S BABY?** ......................................................................................... **74**
    *A letter arrives on 7 May 2015* ........................................................... 76

**2 JUNE 2015 'COURAGE IS A PECULIAR KIND OF FEAR'** ....................... **80**
    ROSE COTTAGE, GOWER.............................................................................. 82

**ANNIVERSARIES** ..................................................................................... **83**

**MINUS ONE** ............................................................................................. **85**
    *July 2016 – Vicargate* .......................................................................... 86

**FEBRUARY 2017** ..................................................................................... **89**
    A STAY OF EXECUTION................................................................................ 92
    MOVING ON?............................................................................................. 94
    NOT GOING ANYWHERE. ............................................................................ 96

**PART 2 - OSCILLATION AND CONFRONTATION** ...................................... **99**

Saturday, 17 March 2018 – Beech House ............................................. 100
Tuesday 25 December 2018 - Beech House – 5.45am ........................ 100

## CHRISTMAS 2010, VICARGATE ............................................. 102

March 2019 ................................................................ 104

## A SHAFT OF LIGHT ............................................................. 107

## 10–18 OCTOBER 2019 – POLO'S TREASURE, VENICE ........................ 110

Croatia ..................................................................... 114

## WHY WE NEED TO REMEMBER ............................................. 118

Dealing with Death ........................................................ 121

## GEORGE ORWELL, WHY I WRITE (1946) ................................... 125

## A SAD DAD ................................................................... 133

## DECEMBER 11TH ............................................................. 139

## WILLIAM 'ERIC' HALL (1938–2020), NEWBIGGIN, 5 FEBRUARY ......... 144

## DENISE ....................................................................... 148

## GRIEF, MELANCHOLIA AND THEORIES – THE SEARCH FOR MEANING . 151

## TICK TOCK ................................................................... 158

## LANDSCAPES ................................................................. 166

## PART 3 - RESTORATION (OF SORTS) ..................................... 174

Death, Grief and Memoir .................................................. 178

## A CREATIVE WRITER'S APPROACH TO DEATH ........................... 183

## WHY? ......................................................................... 187

## DOMINIC – MY SON ........................................................ 189

## END MATTER ................................................................ 194

**HOW IMPORTANT ARE OUR PHOTOS?** ................................................. **195**

**ABOUT THE AUTHOR** .................................................................... **198**

    ACKNOWLEDGEMENTS ............................................................... 199

**APPENDICES** ................................................................................ **200**

    *Appendix 1 Thoughts on a Cumbrian Lad at Bowscale Tarn* ......... 201
    *Appendix 2 Surprised by Joy* ....................................................... 204
    *Appendix 3 On my First Son* ........................................................ 205
    *Appendix 4 The Dash (1996) – by Linda Ellis* ................................ 206
    *Appendix 5 The One I need the Most* .......................................... 208
    *Appendix 6 My Friend* ................................................................. 209
    *Appendix 7 Hope is the Thing with Feathers* ............................... 210
    *Appendix 8 Difficult* .................................................................... 211
    *Appendix 9 More Than a Sonnet.* ................................................ 215
    *Appendix 10 Anthem for Doomed Youth* .................................... 216

**BIBLIOGRAPHY** ............................................................................ **217**

# FOREWORD

Grief has been a preoccupation for philosophers, psychologists and clinicians for over a century. Theories of what it is and how to deal with it have proliferated since then. For me, grief has been my only obsession for the last ten years. On 3 October 2013, my son, Dominic, was killed by a drunk driver. I've been trying to deal with the aftermath of his loss ever since. Psychologists call this process 'meaning making' or 'meaning reconstruction'. In bereavement, this is interpreted as how we try to create new meaning in our lives after our loss. The grieving person often can't return to a pre-loss level of functioning, especially after prolonged or complicated grief, but can learn how to develop a meaningful life without the deceased. Neimeyer, in his *Reconstruction of Meaning* (2011), concludes that this reconstruction is primarily achieved through the use of narratives or life stories.

At the beginning, I had no desire to try to reconstruct my life. Nothing had any value at that point. I started my research and creative journey in the depths of my grief, and despite reading *Grief Counselling and Grief Therapy* (Worden, 2011), which took me to the next level of understanding, it didn't tell me all I wanted to know. The search for books or for information on Google was constant and exhausting. Many sites were a dead end while others helped me to build a multifaceted reading list of grief, including grief memoir. Some were brutally honest, baring their souls and beating their chests. Some writers covered their chests with hair shirts, while others seemed intellectual and cold. I found books that provided some theories and answers, but not a single book that could address all of my thesis questions or, just as important, my own personal questions. I decided that I needed to write one that would.

The book is in three parts entitled 'Loss and Avoidance', 'Oscillation and Confrontation' and 'Restoration (of Sorts)'. The first part of this book is written through the sadness, madness and alcohol-induced nightmare that I found myself in when Dom was killed. The second part tries to intellectualise the first part and metaphorically puts the cork back in the bottle of my grief. Parts two and three are more introspective and it was only at this point that I was able to reflect on and analyse my previous chaotic actions and thoughts following Dom's death. I needed this self-reflection process to at least provide a basic understanding for my psychological fragility. In the long term, it was the writing about Dom's death that helped me to make the connections between my grief and my responses to it.

In his book, Dr Worden writes that in order to live with the loss of someone, there are four things we should try to do. He refers to these things as 'tasks' which are: accept the reality of what's happened, process the pain, adjust to a life without someone's physical presence and create a new connection with them in our memory. Of course, in the depth of your grief, this is easier said than done. Worden's four tasks seemed harsh, perhaps because of the name, they also felt intuitively right, but that path was way in the distant future because of my emotional state at the time. However, the fourth step 'to find an enduring link to the deceased' unknowingly, was the main focus of my memoir, although I didn't connect them together at the time. I called my process 'literary DNA', which is a written acknowledgement between the person who is grieving and the dead. According to Worden, this new connection requires the bereaved person to form an ongoing relationship with their memories of the deceased in such a way that he or she is able to continue with their own life. For me, the best way to do this was to write it down.

Dom and I are chemically intertwined by our biological DNA. Two chains that coil around each other to form a double helix, a combination of cells that contain Susan's and my genetic instructions for Dom's physical development. However, our literary DNA is personal, it is the written words that now also bind us together. It's a term that I started using in 2013 because it can be adopted by everyone wanting to remember a loved one, whether you are biologically connected to them or not, i.e., it could be a person writing about their best friend, a lost pet, or a man about his wife. Literary DNA could be anything from a scribbled note or short memory, a poem, a letter to or from the loved one, or a memoir like this one. This written act of recall or remembrance links them to you forever. Just as important, the very action of putting it down in writing, gives us the survivors, a mental release and a platform to internally commemorate our loved ones.

Throughout the book, I reflect on the work of several famous writers who have also written 'grief memoir', including Joan Didion, CS Lewis and Julian Barnes. I ask why people, particularly writers, write about such a personal thing as grief? Why is their work so important as a form of cultural keening? I was told during my Ph.D. research that 'unfortunately, there is no room for sentimentality or 'sentimental writing' in academia. At the beginning, I found it almost impossible not to write about Dom without a tear in my eye or writing verbose handwringing narrative. It didn't help when I saw no point in continuing my life, wanting to agree a Faustian deal with the devil, or thinking about seeking revenge. So, I also examine my own challenges as a grieving parent trying to write in academia and, deal with the dilemma of trying to remain true to Dominic and my true feelings about his death.

I also read the work of thinkers and writers on grief and death, including Sigmund Freud, Denise Riley and Sir Roger Scruton, plus all the clinicians and psychologists mentioned throughout this book. From this research I took the ex post facto view that psychologists may conclude that we feel sad, angry, depressed or guilty while we are grieving, but, until they've experienced grief personally, they only have theories to try to support you in surviving your pain. Grief is universal – we will all feel its icy touch at some point during our lives – but it affects everyone differently in varying degrees and intensities, all of which are individual and deeply personal. As I wrote Dom's story, I often found myself challenging some of these writers from deep within my own well of pain.

Freud (1918) recommends 'displacement activities' to overcome grief, that is doing something else to take your mind off the pain, such as writing. Some psychologists see this as repressing and ignoring emotions which may be seen as unhealthy. Stroebe and Schut in their *Dual Process model* (1999) believe that for most people avoiding these deep emotions is a normal way of coping with grief. They argue that numerous internal post-traumatic stresses come into play during grief. Therefore, grief is an inimitable experience and theories of grief and bereavement like the Dual Process model can help to consolidate ideas about how people think they should deal with the death of a loved one. The theories of psychologists such as Dr Kübler Ross and Worden also argue that grief has to be 'worked through' or 'faced head on'. Stroebe and Schut do not believe this is true. They agree with Freud and suggest that sometimes ignoring your emotions, or distracting yourself from your grief, is a natural way of coping with it. While bereavement is a universal phenomenon, individual experience of grief is not.

The ongoing philosophical, psychological and clinical debate about grief highlights that a death can be simply too big for our minds to take in all at once. Learning to adapt to life without the dead can be very hard. Experts have defined emotional phases, which may come in waves, go around in circles or seem like steps to which we can return to as we adjust to a new but acceptable life without that someone we love. Grief models are developed to try to help people work through the grieving process, and to reassure them that what they are going through is 'normal'. Processing grief in this way is essentially described as a journey towards the acknowledgement of loss rather than a 'cure'. Much of the narrative in this book revolves around this premise. It examines how other writers process their grief through their memoirs, novels or songs, but as an autoethnographical work, it narrates my own grief while drawing comparisons with these other contributors.

Grief is a complicated and an individual process. Alluding to patterns of 'normal' behaviour, as many theories do, doesn't account for the exclusiveness of each person's bereavement. The flow of the narrative in this book is grief, and alcohol-fuelled, at least at the start. It contains descriptions of bereavement from other writers in several genres and also in pain. These images are segued with some of my own diary entries over a seven-year period.

Ultimately, the backdrop of the memoir becomes the story of a lonely man, trying to find solace in his son's death, desperately trying not to forget his son's smile.

## Note to the Reader

You will have noticed I mentioned autoethnography. I refer to it several other times throughout the memoir so I thought I'd nail that one straight away. Autoethnography is a research method that intertwines personal experiences with cultural analysis. In the context of my Ph.D. research, I employed autoethnography as a means to delve deeply into my own life experiences while critically examining the broader societal and cultural contexts that shaped them. This approach allowed me to connect my personal journey to larger themes, shedding light on the universal through the personal.

After my academic journey, I transformed these autoethnographic explorations into a compelling narrative, effectively transcribing the raw data of my experiences into a memoir. By doing so, I not only bridged the gap between academic inquiry and storytelling but also offered readers an authentic and unfiltered account of this part of mine and Dom's journey. In essence, my memoir serves as a tribute to the power of autoethnography to bring the truth of one's experiences to light, making it accessible and relatable to a wider audience.

The use of autoethnography not only enriches the academic discourse with personal insights but also brings the often-hidden complexities of human experiences to a broader readership. This fusion of scholarship and storytelling allows for a deeper, more engaging exploration of the truth, transcending the confines of traditional research and making my work accessible and impactful to you, the reader.

# Part 1 - Loss and Avoidance

# Didn't you used to be Ian Loftus?

'Charlie, move over and let the gentleman sit down, please.'

I smile at the woman and wink at the little girl as she shuffles along the faux leather bench to make space for me. Her eyes don't leave mine. Suspicious, she searches for her mother's hand. The mother smiles back and draws the child closer.

I don't recognise anyone in the waiting room. A man looks vaguely in my direction, but quickly looks down again, just in time. He's wearing a bow tie and I do a double take. He looks familiar, but do I know anyone who wears a bow tie? I pick up 'Cumbrian Life' from the coffee table; it feels expensive and informative in my hand but I can only see the main strapline. I pretend to read for a couple of minutes and put it back. Shall I get my reading glasses from the car? Yes, I've got time before my appointment. It's snowing outside, but not 'real snow', not like when we were kids.

\*\*\*

The thin cane meets little resistance as it draws another fine red welt across the fingers on my upturned right hand.

'That's six,' says Mr Roberts. Did he think I would lose count?

He looks down at me, his hands and the weapon held guiltily behind his back. My left hand is still held behind mine. A curtain of moisture is hanging over my eyes, but I meet his gaze and try to look in control.

'You're not going to throw snowballs at buses in the future are you, Loftus?' he says softly.

'No, sir.' Tears run down my face, more from shame than from the pain.

He places the cane next to the mortarboard on his desk and opens the door for me. His gown billows in the draught from the corridor. I step through the opening, my left hand hugging the right. The draught blows my long hair into my face and it is comforting. It hides my damp piggy eyes from any potential pisstakers passing by.

'Right, Ian, back to French, and good luck tonight.'

At the sound of my Christian name and the thought of playing rugby later I turn to thank him, the painful digits almost forgotten. But the headmaster's door is already closed. I never did throw snowballs at buses again.

I kick the toes of my shoes against the surgery doorstep to shake off the snow and return to the waiting room. The man with the bow tie has gone but has been replaced by a young woman holding a child, rocking it gently. I sit down and put my glasses case down beside me on the bench. No-one speaks so I search the floor for a piece of carpet to claim as mine. An errant snowflake has attached itself to my shoelace.

Last week we had 'real snow' again, flakes the size of slices of French bread. Wednesday, a metre overnight, each snowfall displayed layer by layer on the chalet roofs like the age circles of a tree. With skis over my shoulder and heels digging in the snow long before my toes did, I walked John-Cleese-like off the piste and into the car park. Our chalet in Morzine was only a moment from the Pleney Gondola but on the flip side it was on the corner of two busy thoroughfares. Outside our kitchen window was the main bus terminus to Avoriaz. Every evening as the piste emptied, families and groups of skiers would come and go as the buses ghosted silently up through the snowy grey tracks, then left with a whoosh as they continued the silent run down the 'rue'. In between buses, the passengers would stand beneath our kitchen window, discussing the 'rouge' and the 'noire' they'd conquered that day.

I crossed the road and turned left, goose stepping down the side of the chalet. A group of French teenagers aged between thirteen and sixteen had spilled onto our terrace from the bus queue and were having a late afternoon snack. Some sat in the snow with their backs to the wall, eating and laughing. A couple were having a snowball fight, and the rest were trying to look into one of our chalet windows.

I turned left again and went through the garage under the chalet and into the dry room. I eased my ankles out of boots that were a dominatrix dream. It seemed I was the last one back. My socks soaked up the melted snow left by the other boots warming on the heaters. I heard giggles from upstairs and followed the happy sound, leaving soggy footprints on the marble steps. I was wrong; none of the adults were back and I could see why the kids outside were trying to look in through the window. Reuben, the youngest of the English chalet defenders, was wearing an England Rugby shirt: the red rose on the front, his pride, the tiny Saint George's cross on the back, his rallying symbol. He had a mop bucket full of snow. The French kids had jumped to their feet, food and drinks forgotten. Although there was an abundance of snow, they jostled to grab fistfuls. Almost in unison, a hail of snowballs hit the balcony above me and I heard Reuben scrambling to hide. I placed a tea towel over my arm like a waiter, grabbed the shopping list and pen from the counter and opened the terrace door.

'Messieurs-dames, vous desirez?' My accent wasn't perfect.

All motion on the terrace stopped; I felt just like the stranger who'd entered the saloon in an old cowboy movie. Suddenly, the French kids got the joke and I only had time to put the tea towel on my head before the next barrage of snowballs hit me and the chalet.

\*\*\*

The waiting room door opens and a young man walks in, closely followed by a woman with a face like fried fat. I assume she's his mother. He's got one arm in the sleeve of a duffle coat and the other in a makeshift sling; I can make out the words 'Typhoo Tea' and realise his sling is really a tea towel. Beneath the coat he wears the black and white rugby shirt of the Newcastle Falcons. He's very slight in build and doesn't look like a rugby player so I wonder how he's hurt his arm.

\*\*\*

'Great tackle, Loftus.'

Mr Baker, the rugby teacher, beams at me. My pinstripe fingers had long been forgotten.

At aged fourteen that was the life: I played for the school first fifteen, had permission to leave school early and the last two periods that day were Maths. Result! It didn't get any better than that.

'Loftus, take a piece of orange and pass them on. There's only a quarter each, mind.' Mr Baker thrusts a plastic bag into my hands and I dig in.

A man in a long grey coat comes over from the far touchline.

'That was a fantastic tackle, young man.'

I wasn't listening; the orange is the most exotic thing I've ever seen. I'd tasted nothing like it before.

'Are you talking to any of the local clubs?' He dips into Mr Baker's bag of oranges.

'No, sir. Do you know that's an orange?'

He smiled at me and sucks the flesh from the orange skin in one go.

'What's your name, son?' He spits out a pip.

'It's Ian, Ian Loftus, sir.'

'I'll remember that,' he says, and walks back to the visitor's touchline.

But I didn't listen. I was only fourteen, Mark Bolan and T Rex were a zillion times more important than rugby and I'd just eaten my first orange. Later that year I swam a mile in my pyjamas, had my first pint of bitter, got to third base with a girl called 'Hedgehog' and believed I could leap tall buildings in a single bound.

\*\*\*

'Great tackle, Loftus.'

I moved too quickly and winced at the sharp pain in my neck. The rugby teacher wasn't booming at me; he was shouting at Dom. Despite the pain I remembered well that feeling of exhilaration playing rugby; I made my own contribution to the noise.

'Low and hard, Dom, low and hard.'

'Hi. Are you Dominic's dad?' A large lady breathed garlic in my face and I took an involuntary step back. I nodded enthusiastically, not breathing in.

'Thought so. I saw you with him at parents' evening. Has he made his GCSE choices yet?'

Despite her huge frame, her bright red Dare2B ski jacket was still two sizes too big and I could just see her little Gortex fingers poking out from the bottom of the sleeve.

'Yes, he's quite keen to...' I started to breathe out.

'He's a lovely boy, and my Robert said he played a blinder at Queen Elizabeth Grammar last week. Anyway, nice to meet you. Bye.'

She waddled off down the touch line, her legs and her own breath laboured at the effort. I breathed in the freshly mown grass of the rugby pitch.

\*\*\*

'Excuse me, have you got this in a medium?'

The sales assistant took the XXL from me, expertly flicked through the rail and pulled out a medium within seconds.

'Medium!' she said, and handed me the Berghaus jacket in such a way that I felt like a careless school boy who'd misplaced his pencil case.

She gave me the 'Typical man!' look and started up a conversation with a female customer further down the aisle. She said something and they both looked at me, nodding sagely.

'Excuse me, aren't you Susan's husband?' The customer moved in my direction.

'Yes.' My name's Ian.

'I've seen your picture in the paper. You're an Eden District councillor, aren't you?'

'Was! I did my four years and left.'

'Ah, the snake's pit! You either survive or you get eaten alive.' She nodded sagely again.

I half agreed, 'I just didn't feel like I was making a diff...'

'Nice jacket. You off skiing, then?' She spoke over me, not really expecting an answer.

\*\*\*

I felt the cool vanilla roundness of the snowball again as I moulded it to the shape of my cupped hand. A French boy's head and shoulders bobbed up and down above the chalet's perimeter wall. My snowball met little resistance through the thin air; it splattered harmlessly against the wall and he ducked. Laughter sounds the same in any language. I scooped up another ice cream cone of snow. Thirty-nine years later, was Mr Roberts watching the Portes du Soleil bus route? My aim wasn't good, but Reuben's snowball connected with one of the French invaders every time. They knew his name and shouted, 'Rudy, Rudy, monsieur Rudy!'

\*\*\*

'You're Reuben's dad, aren't you?'

'Yes,' I said quickly at the unexpected voice. Yes, I am Reuben's dad but my name's Ian, Ian Loftus. I placed my pint back down on the bar, 'Do I...?'

'You don't remember me, I can tell. But it's okay.'

I looked hard at her face. She was right; I didn't. Angling my head to one side, I feigned faint recognition.

'Why would you? I was fifteen; you were twenty-five and some kind of a god.'

I looked harder and vaguely recollected her eyes.

'You had that beautiful white car with two doors – what was it now?'

'It was a Ford Escort, one point one litre popular.' I tried to make it sound grander than it was; she encouraged my memory with another teaser.

'My mum was the barmaid in the Gloucester Arms and I waited on tables at the weekends?'

I was in the bar every weekend with my friends, but I couldn't remember her face; in fact, I couldn't remember some of my old friends' faces now.

'I tried to talk to you but I couldn't breathe, especially when I got close enough to speak. You never saw me.' All the time her eyes never left mine.

I searched my memory for a potential asthmatic stalker; our eyes had held for far too long and I had started to admire this straight-talking middle-aged woman. Despite her fond and flattering memories, I didn't think she could remember my name either.

\*\*\*

'Ian Loftus?' The surgery assistant has appeared at the door.

'That's me,' I say in my head.

No-one in the waiting room looks up from their patch of pattern on the carpet. I look at Charlie, one hand now tucked under her leg and her head in her mother's lap. She looks up at me. I must seem like a giant to her from that angle. She presses herself against her mother on the bench. I catch her eye, start to smile but stop myself.

'Yes, that's me,' I answer, and in my head Ian, Ian Peter Loftus. I've got a badge for swimming a mile in my pyjamas. Still, no-one looks up.

I walk towards the door. I'm almost level with the assistant when I feel a tug on my jacket.

'You forgot your glasses, Ian Loftus.' Charlie reaches up to me holding the case in both hands, her suspicions gone. Back to her mother's side searching for the hand again, her eyes never left mine.

>Dr Arora is a petite woman, 'What can I do for you this morning, Mr Loftus?'
>
>'Do you believe in miracles, Doctor?'
>
>She sits back in her chair, her eyes dart to the big red panic button. She humours me,
>
>'It depends really, why?'
>
>I think of Charlie cuddling her mum outside. 'After all these years, I seem to have regained the ability to leap tall buildings in a single bound'.

# Narrow Field of Vision

The twenty milligrams of temazepam has done its job. Susan's pain has left her for a few hours as the drugs take the weight of Dominic's death off her shoulders. The duvet moves up and down slowly. As I watch, I can't help but ask myself a thousand questions. How will my pain end? If God doesn't exist, or if I don't believe in God, will the pain ever end?

Dominic has no pain. A car spins out of control and demolishes a wall. He's in the back, laughing. He doesn't know he's dead. I'm tempted to reach for the temazepam too, but I know they won't work. The black Zippo lighter Dom carried in his pocket that night is now in my hand. I find myself wanting to touch something he has touched. I need to feel comfort in the smoothness of the undamaged casing. In the darkness, the flame that never blows out even in the wind kills my night vision. I snap the lid closed again. The light, my sight, extinguished. If God does exist, hallelujah, I think bitterly. I will recant, and an unseen, bright new chapter will be started; my dearly departed son will have entered the next life, one the living will never know. The living are left in perpetual pain. We cry each day with the guilt of breathing, eating and seeing the sun still shine. Anger. Helplessness. Loss. We will live the rest of our lives with that most common of post-traumatic stress disorders: Grief.

If I recant my beliefs will that end my pain?

My unshaven chin scrapes the sheet. It sounds like the footfall of the legion of mourners who slowly shuffled down the church aisle on 18 October 2013. My wife's breath goes in and out. If I exhale and stop, it will all be over. If I don't breathe in again, the gap, where my heart used to be, will no longer exist. If I stop breathing, the re-run of Dominic's life without sound, the re-run of the spinning car, will end too.

The void seems to be filling, but not with oxygen. I can hear a vacuum cleaner in another room, also fading. It seems to be sucking the air from my lungs, slowly. I see myself in a different vacuum, floating above the bed. In thirty seconds, I will know how the philosophical argument concludes. I will know if Dominic is waiting somewhere for me to join him. Vicarious atonement? A field of reeds? Re-born with no memory of a previous life? Or is there simply no electrical activity in a cold cortex? If I stop breathing, who will fetch the logs in the rain and snow? Who will split the kindling? Who will cook the beef bourguignon on Christmas Eve? Who will do all the driving and the school runs?

Who will remember Dominic?

The blind is suddenly ruffled by a breeze from the open window. I hear his voice

'Don't be a bloody idiot, Ian.' Susan breathes in and out. Slowly, with regret, I too inhale. The feeling of helplessness returns.

***

'Have you got a loved one buried here?'

A woman is holding the hand of a young man with Down's syndrome. He swishes a broken tree branch like a lightsaber.

'No. Not yet. Perhaps next week.'

'You must be from the cottage?' The woman blocks another arc of the wooden lightsaber. 'Tom, please,' she soothes. 'War should be the only reason a parent buries their child.'

'Hello, Tom.' The man touches the boy's arm. 'Do you like your walks down to the church?'

Tom swishes again and the man lets him. 'There are some very old people down here, Tom. Not many your age.'

'I still speaks to them, tho.' Tom strokes the man's arm. 'Died in the war, you know.' His head sunk back; he squints towards the church's twin bell tower. The excess skin on the back of his neck becomes thicker.

'Do they talk back to you, Tom?'

'Yeah. Soldiers.' His tree branch hums as it becomes a lightsaber once more.

***

The bench made of cast iron is lipstick red. I don't have a jacket, the station doesn't have a roof, I don't feel the cold. A yellow line runs the length of the platform. On the other side of the station, the green camouflage gear looks odd in the poor lighting. The young squaddie seems superimposed on the backdrop of the ticket office. Clearly, he's packed for a very long journey.

'The next train arriving on Platform Two is the 8.30 to Glasgow.' Pause. 'The 8.20 Virgin Pendolino to Edinburgh will not be stopping. Please stand well back from the platform.' Open mic feedback, then click. The announcer, also the Station Master, appears on Platform One directly below the meter-wide digital clock. It reads 20:19:25.

The yellow line is only two feet from the track. In thirty-five seconds, a train will travel at 125 miles per hour two feet from the yellow line. There are many natural dualities, light and dark, hot and cold, fire and water, life and death, all physical manifestations of yin-yang. Ten thousand tons of steel, including the buffet car, and one hundred and twenty-five pounds of human flesh, are opposing forces and not complimentary. It may end the pain. A shadow cannot exist without light. Can I exist without him?

I stand as the train becomes visible in the distance. The soldier also turns to face the track. The digital clock above his head now reads 20:19:45. I take a step towards the yellow line. 20:19:50. The soldier senses my movement and faces me fully, dropping his rucksack. The shoulder strap catches something red on his chest and it flutters to the ground. He is still looking at me. I point to the fallen object as I step forward. He picks it up and shows me a thumb. He holds out a poppy with the other hand. He disappears with the flash, flash, flash of the train. The clock reads 20:20:10 as the disappearing Edinburgh Pendolino reveals the smiling soldier again across the track.

***

The physical presence, the shell, wrapped in oak, padded in satin and lace, looks asleep. There's a smell of burning candle wax, but no music. I always imagined that there would be music. I wrote a letter yesterday and now slip it into Dominic's shirt pocket. Susan chose his favourite shirt: the one with buttoned-down breast pockets. There are two other letters, both folded neatly, one on lined paper, one on plain. There are some coins and a £5 note.

'It's a bugger', the funeral director said.

\*\*\*

In pictures around the house, the physical body grows from room to room; from a few minutes old covered in after-birth, the one-year-old with food on his face, the boy in a school tie, blazer and with missing teeth, the youth in a base-ball cap, to the man, taller than his parents with a beer in his hand. I don't need the pictures to see or feel the virtual beauty, the unfailing smile, the ungainly gait, the blue eyes, the mole on the forehead. The way he held his left arm when he was thinking or talking. I don't need the pictures to remember the uncontrollable desire to please, the loyalty to friends and family, the inner beauty; innocence, gentleness, thoughtfulness and honesty. His heart and his intentions. What has happened to that individual, the bespoke entity and the emotional bundle that made him who he was? His energy and his consciousness, these just can't die with the shell.

In my heart, I want to believe in an angel on a fluffy cloud playing a harp, but my head is telling me something else. Is this entity I can no longer touch or hear or smell, the principle of life, the feeling, the thought and the action of him, still regarded as a distinct entity, separate in existence from his body? Or is the afterlife just a story made up before Socrates' time by a fallen soldier's wife to comfort their child?

\*\*\*

Despite the driving wind the water of Bowscale Tarn is flat. It's protected by Carrock Fell on my right and Combe Height and Knott to the front. There is inescapable evidence on Facebook that Dom made this walk many times with Lucy, his border collie. I hear him call her to heel despite the howling easterly storm. His voice, a thousand times sharper than the cutting wind, slices to my heart. My chest, gossamer thin, is no protection.

The water is black, bottomless as the local myth goes. The myth also tells of two immortal fish, one given the power of speech. I stand at the water's edge, drawn to its limitlessness. In my insanity I call the fish to heel, again and again. I step out onto the first exposed stone in the water. Against the wind I call the fish again. I scan the water for a sign and step to the next visible stone. Now a foot on each one, the water still, calm and inviting, I try to fathom its depths. A few lines from a Wordsworth's poem bounce and echo around the fell, or is it my head? The Cumbrian accent cuts even deeper.

> And both the undying fish that swim,
> through Bowscale-Tarn did wait on him,
> the pair were servants of his eye in their immortality,
> they moved about in open sight,
> to and fro, for his delight.
>
> 'Song at the Feast of Brougham Castle' (1888)

One more step, there are no more stones. The wind has dropped, Wordsworth is silent. I could dive into the blankness, and hold onto the tail of the immortal fish, swimming to eternity, to the bottom that doesn't exist. I won't hear his voice again, only the talking fish.

*** 

'Hello, Tom, good to see you again.' The boy's narrow eyes, bare of colour, look to a space beyond the churchyard. He moves closer to his mother. The man from the cottage points to a fresh grave in the direction close to where they are walking. 'Can you see where the flowers are, Tom? There's a young man there; he's about your age.'

Tom's gaze shifts to the light brown wooden cross. 'Soldier?' he asks.

'No, Tom.' The man looks at the cross too. 'He loved to play 'Call of Duty' on his Xbox, though. He never did read Sun Tzu.'

Colourless eyes re-focus on something a thousand yards away.

'When you take your walks will you say hello to him for me?' The man touches the wooden cross. 'I'm not sure if I'll be back again.'

'Poppy. Can I put it with the other flowers?' Tom exposes a gap between his two front teeth as he smiles. He spins the plastic stalk between his fingers. It drops onto the grass as he holds out the red flower to show the man.

'Very pretty, Tom. He never went to Flanders either, but I'm sure he would like that.' The man takes a pen and a note pad from his wax jacket. He writes quickly, tears out a sheet of paper, folds it and gives it to Tom.

'Can you put this next to your poppy, Tom? Perhaps you and your mum can write it out every year for him?'

Tom's mum takes the folded sheet. She holds the man's elbow and smiles. Tom looks up the steep church lane.

'What says, Mum?'

Her gaze never leaves the man walking across the grass. As she unfolds the paper the man closes the church gate behind him. The winter sun casts long shadows across the pasture to High Pike, Carrock, Mosedale, Mungrisdale and to the church at his back. The man's shadow moves slowly across the grave, the flowers, the wooden cross, and falls at the gate. He walks up the narrow tree-lined lane, not looking back, his shadow in sync with the low October morning light, his hand in his pocket.

'It's a poem, Tom, a poem about soldiers and flowers, just like yours. Listen.'

>In Flanders fields the poppies blow
>Between the crosses, row on row,
>That mark our place: and in the sky
>The larks, still bravely singing, fly
>Scarce heard amid the guns below.
>We are the Dead. Short days ago
>We lived, felt dawn, saw sunset glow,
>Loved, and were loved, and now we lie
>In Flanders fields.
>J.M.

\*\*\*

I never saw Tom and his mother again, but writing in the third person somehow gave me some distance and allowed me to write about them and about Dom. It's the first literary connection with Dom since his death. My university supervisor liked one of the scenes and suggested that I try to make a poem from it. I'm not a poet, but just the fact that I associate Dominic with Bowscale Tarn, and therefore Wordsworth, meant I needed to try. I wrote 'Thoughts on a Cumbrian Lad at Bowscale' (Appendix 1).

Wordsworth himself was no stranger to the early death of a child. During his marriage to Mary Hutchinson, he had five children between 1803 and 1810. Three of the children predeceased both parents: Thomas, aged six, Catherine, aged three, and Dora, aged forty-three. When Dora died in 1847, Wordsworth was devastated and stopped writing poetry. This contradicts my belief that writing and creativity can help us through grief. On the other hand, for Wordsworth it might just have been the final straw. Dora died only three years before his own death, aged eighty.

It was Catherine, however, who had the biggest impact on Wordsworth emotionally and, I would argue, on his creativity. 'Surprised by Joy' (Appendix 2) is Wordsworth's heart-breaking sonnet which begins in joy and ends in sorrow. At the beginning, following Catherine's death, the first time he experiences joy, Wordsworth is surprised by a feeling he never expected to experience again. He quickly turns to share it with someone, but that someone has gone. 'I turned to share the transport—Oh! with whom but thee, long buried in the silent Tomb.' I pick up the phone to call Dom all the time, his number is still in my mobile, only to realise he isn't there anymore. How could I even contemplate deleting it?

Wordsworth too realises that Catherine isn't there and won't ever be there again. He is acutely aware of his grief. It sweeps over him, blotting out any hint of earlier joy. He seems to experience the shock of loss all over again just as it had consumed him when he first heard the news of her death. 'Surprised by Joy' ends with the realisation that his joy would always be swept away in grief, because no amount of time could ever bring back to him that 'heavenly face' which he was missing so dearly.

Poets seem to be well equipped to capture their grief in their words. Two hundred years earlier, in 1603, Ben Johnson wrote his elegy 'On My First Son' (Appendix 3) following the death of his seven-year-old boy from the plague. In the poem, Johnson struggles to answer the questions that Wordsworth and I also couldn't answer: Can he recover from this hammer blow? And if he can, what could possibly compensate him for the loss? The death of Dora stops Wordsworth writing. After Benjamin dies Johnson vows never to love anything ever again. I find myself at the edge of Bowscale Tarn looking for the impossible, improbable immortal fish. Again, I'm not a poet. I'm not famous. How can I write meaningfully and passionately about my son's death? What clever, or even weaselly, words can I weave together that will bring him back to life?

# The Good Old Days

Before 3 October 2013, we were a normal family. On one hand, stressed because we had been renovating Vicargate since December 1987. Our remote cottage, barn and small holding had turned out to be a seventeenth century money pit. On the other, we were totally blessed because it was located in the wildest and most beautiful part of the English Lake District.

The family became five quickly with our three children arriving throughout the 90s, and country life was good but hard work. I had a job based in London for most of the time, so as the children got older, we taught them to share the load and they grew up quickly.

By the start of the millennium, renovation work on the cottage had progressed and Susan and I could sit on our new terrace sipping wine. We watched the children play as the sun slowly sank behind High Pike, a fell south of Caldbeck. We could see seven or eight miles towards those western fells, and several clear miles north and south. I would light a citronella candle just as the other isolated homestead lights came on. The lights acknowledged the farmers' continued survival across the valley despite two bouts of Foot and Mouth Disease in a generation.

As the light faded, the children went to bed one by one in order of age, Dom getting an extra ten minutes to play after the other two had gone.

After seventeen years at Vicargate, the routine with the children changed. As soon as he could, Dominic left home to travel, though I imagined at some point in the future that he would return and have his own family. One sultry night, the fellside farms blinking across the mountains and pregnant bats silent on the warm wind, he would gently shake me awake and tell me it was time to put my grandchildren to bed. That's what I expected, anyway.

Our nearest neighbours to the north, Simon and Annette, were half a mile away and St Kentigern's church, the nearest structure to the south, was hidden by woods a few fields away. I only mention this because one time in the spring of 1990, Susan and I lay on the grass in the orchard enjoying the sunshine and made love right there underneath a cherry tree, knowing we wouldn't be overlooked by our neighbours. When four-foot snow drifts blocked our drive later that year, Susan, eight months pregnant with Dominic, walked the third of a mile up to the public road carrying my wellington boots. I'd made it to the top of our road but couldn't drive or walk any further. I'd left home earlier that week, dressed in a pinstripe suit and brogues, but no coat and gloves. Even then, in the blinding snowstorm, the location was sublime.

Everything changed early that morning on 4 October 2013. I was in bed. Susan screamed for me to come downstairs. The flashing blue light I could see through the hall window was startling in an area without street lights for miles in any direction. Two policemen in high visibility jackets stood in the doorway. In the living room, they asked us to sit down. My heart is pounding even now as I write this. Dominic had been involved in an accident at 10.30 pm the night before. The driver and two other passengers were in intensive care, but Dom had been killed. Three, short, sentences and then a life sentence.

I had started my Masters in Writing at Liverpool John Moores University (LJMU) the day before and had driven two hundred and fifty miles there and back to attend my first lecture. We had a late supper. As the policemen left through the kitchen, there were no sounds. I couldn't even hear Susan sobbing for her boy any more. The flashing blue lights drowned out our previous life. I saw the unwashed dinner plates in the sink. Without warning, the forlorn hopes, 'les enfant perdus', struck me hard with their first assault. They will be relentless over the coming years, taking me down with a thousand guilts, the death of a thousand cuts. That first guilt? How could I have been enjoying a steak while Dom lay dead, upside down in a ditch?

After the police left, we set off immediately back down to LJMU to try to speak with our daughter, Chloe. We wanted to see her before Dom's death hit social media. Chloe had started her Criminology and Psychology degree at the university the month before me and was still finding her feet. We drove down in silence. Reuben, aged fifteen, was in the back seat, dazed, not really knowing what was happening.

We arrived at 8.45 am, but we were too late. Chloe was standing on the street outside her halls with her bags at her feet, her eyes deep red and underlined by half-moon black shadows. She already knew her brother was dead; it was on Facebook.

# 9th October 2013

Throughout 2012 and 2013 Dom lived in his own flat above one of the family businesses. He owned and drove his own car for pleasure and he had a van for work. He was a young man but he had personal affairs that still needed to be organised. His mobile phone contract and car insurance had to be stopped, his bank accounts frozen, bills paid. His border collie, Lucy, was rehomed. Susan and Chloe spent most of today in his now empty flat reorganising and slowly cancelling his life.

# 11th October 2013

'Hello, Mr. Loftus, its Phil, family liaison officer. Dom's possessions have been released; can I bring them to you?'

'Yes.'

'One other thing. Can I suggest you write your own announcement for the local press?'

'I'm not sure. Can't you do it for us?'

'What the press don't know they'll make up. They'll take pictures and comments out of context from Facebook or other social media. I think you should provide your own if you feel strong enough?'

We've all heard the story of the mother lifting up the back of a car because her child is trapped underneath. Where did that mother's strength come from? She didn't know or care; she just knew she had to save her baby. I don't know if my mind cleared just for that moment or it was in autopilot, but I knew I didn't want the newspapers to write about Dom. They didn't know him. I found something from somewhere and I told Cumbria who he was.

# 14th October 2013 – The Westmorland Herald

They say just before you die your life flashes before your eyes. What they don't say is that when someone very close to you dies their life flashes before your eyes. Dominic's twenty-two years have been on 'shuffle' in my head since 6.30am, 4 October, after the police arrived to tell us the news. His life is now a playlist on the hard drive in my head. Susan knew straight away. Two policemen in high viz at the door before 6.30 in the morning?

I only know what 'shuffle' means because Dominic has tried to persuade me to get an iPhone for the last five or six years. I finally gave in, in July 2013. Now added to Dominic's 'playlist' are other flashes of his life, or his death; a grainy snapshot of our twenty-two-year-old son, dead, on a table in Carlisle hospital.

Then, flash, I see the time he came home with his dog Lucy, with a big grin on his face. 'She's a beast', he said. In reality she was a fluffy black and white border collie he'd been given by his pal, Ollie. From that moment, Lucy never left his side.

I see a constant beaming white smile, like a toothpaste advertisement interspersed between the flashes of Dominic's life. 'You're an idiot, Ian', he would say, smiling. He only called me Dad in private; he thought Ian was more professional. The same smile was there earlier this year when we went to collect his Mazda 6 MPS with his friend Tom. As he drove back from Edinburgh in it, he smiled all the way. The last time I saw Dominic alive was the morning of 3 October when we dropped off some kind of 'widget' at the garage to fit to the Mazda. It would make the engine on his car do something better, I never knew what, but he had the same big smile when he dropped me off at home that same morning.

'See ya later, Dad.'

I did, but he was dead. I saw him the next day, lying on a mortuary table at Carlisle Hospital. His smile can never leave me.

The next flash was when his mum and I dropped him at Manchester Airport to fly to Lanzarote to work. He had a great time on the Canary Islands, learning about the pub and restaurant business. But, typical Dominic, he spoke to or texted us every day. He loved his iPhone and he used it for everything listening to music, running his business, texting and email.

Dominic went to Fellview School at Caldbeck and then on to Ullswater High School in 2002. I have another flash of him breaking a rib on the South African school rugby tour, learning later he broke it falling over in the shower, not playing rugby. Seeing his smile when he came home from the tour and gave us the African 'Family Symbol' painting. The painting still has pride of place on the living room wall.

We spent hours one day in 2005 looking through our cookery books trying to find recipes for a couple of dishes he could make. He entered in the 'ready steady cook' inter-school challenge between Queen Elizabeth and Ullswater Schools and came second. He could cook well, and he did it all throughout 2013, helping out in both our restaurants. We don't know how we would have managed without him. What now is the next memory, for tomorrow? 'What are we going to do without Dominic?'

Whilst Dom loved cooking, it wasn't as much fun or as interesting as getting his hands and knees dirty. He climbed through a lot of loft spaces to run electrical wiring, he loved working out a problem on a fuse board, running some new lights into a farmer's barn or putting his mind to just about anything practical. I remember watching him when he was four. I looked out of the window one summer morning as he hammered a nail through a piece of wood without missing a stroke.

On the other hand, I remember him skiing more on his backside than on his skis, but I think that was more just for the comedy value.

There aren't enough column inches to describe Dominic and how we remain so proud of him and his energy and his zest for life. He couldn't sit still. He was always wanting to do something. He even got bored on Christmas Day.

Dom liked a pint with his pals, young and old. The younger ones have just had their first pool game as the Sportsmans team this last week. They lost, of course, but they still enjoyed each other's company. I guess the main topic of conversation after the game would have been 'The Glendale', a campervan they joint owned, and a 'doer-upper'.

One day when he was eighteen, we drove into Penrith in his car. It seemed every other car flashed, or its passengers waved at us: every person we passed on the street said 'Hi', smiled, joked or spoke with him. I didn't know until then how popular he was and how many people knew and liked him. Even on the morning he died, many of his friends and associates had gathered at the Sportsmans Inn by 11 am.

***

Phil gave me Dom's possessions back yesterday. I held everything in my hand, and then I wrote a poem. Haiku is a short poem with just three lines. It's more than a genre of poetry; it is a way of looking at the very nature of existence. Haiku has been called 'unfinished' poetry because each one requires the reader to finish it in his or her heart.

    Dominic would hate me writing that too; he had no interest in anything that was seen as highbrow, cultural or even art. He loved hip hop, particularly the rapper Eminem. I wonder, would Dom argue that was art? Rap music usually has a message with simple, rhyming lyrics to a loud bass rhythm, unlike Haiku, a three-line stanza that traditionally doesn't rhyme.

## L o s t   k e y s

> Selfless, simpleness,
> A backseat, thoughtfulness,
> leaves us, without reason…

# 18 October 2013 – St Andrew's Church – Penrith

Dom's funeral service was arranged by Susan, Chloe and Reuben, with a eulogy from Linzi. They chose the songs, Reuben wrote and performed his own song, and they designed the order of service with photos. When I stand up in front of the rest of Dom's family and his friends, what can I say to comfort them? In their hearts and minds, they need to finish Dom's haiku, they need to insert their own memories and words to remember him by. What seed can I plant for them to write their own ending to his story? For me I can't see an end.

How can I start to describe the omnipresent young man who is my son? He is everywhere. The ubiquitous nature of his life, his talent and personality can be seen wherever I look. The chippings on the drive that he spread with his friends, the wiring behind the TV when he 'sorted out' the Sky box, the lights in the hall, the crème brûlée dishes he sent me a picture of from his phone just before he bought them. Everything I see, hear, smell or touch reminds me of Dominic. Even as I type these words, he's here, every app, every song and picture on my iPad. He put the zigzag screen protector on for me as we sat in the office a few months ago, and then, he showed me where the on button was.

As he grew from the floppy-fringed blond 'Smiler', my nickname for him as a boy, to the gentle young man he is today, he became and was a man for all seasons: eventually the tragic hero, but before that a man who had the ability to mix seamlessly with all people regardless of age, sex, creed or colour. He could be effing and blinding drinking beer with his pals, or having a nice cup of tea with an old lady, drinking it cold because she'd forgotten to boil the kettle. Then he'd fit her storage heater and do any other jobs she wanted done while he was there, all for ten quid.

Later in the day he would be the professional businessman. He'd deal firmly with a poor supplier – even in his hoodie – then chef, sending out a hundred meals in three hours. At the end of a hard day in the kitchen, he could charm the birds right off the trees from behind the bar, then lock the doors and party all night with his friends.

I was privileged to have known him as a man. He had firmly established views on many subjects, including immigration, children, God and Vodafone, and we discussed these and lots of other ideas on many occasions. I won't share his views but I'm proud to say, whether I agreed with him or not, that he formed his opinions with conviction and he would defend them with robust discussion. He wasn't academic. We never discussed art or poetry, but he knew about music, technology and the day-to-day practicalities of living a country life. I'm not ashamed to say he instinctively knew more about friendship, loyalty and when and how to do the 'right thing', whatever the situation than I do. He never cared about money, as long as he had enough to pay his round at the bar and pay his bills. He hated owing anyone anything.

I used to worry about him when he was younger. He didn't want the things that I wanted for him: doctor, lawyer or to be a six-figure earner. We had many heated words about that at the time. He hated school and couldn't wait to leave. He was right of course; he followed his own path and achieved a great deal over a short period. He was very content with his life and didn't ask for much. He was a man of simple pleasures and he was satisfied by the ordinary things in life. The less complicated the better. A new pair of Nike Airs made his year and he counted down the days until he could 'upgrade' his phone. He loved going to 'Mackie D's' for a double cheese burger, or 'Deniz's' for a kebab. The simple things that I took as a given, made him happy or made him smile that big contagious grin. Throughout his life, man and boy, he had no pretensions and when he wanted or bought anything, he did so because he liked it or it did what he needed it to do. He never wanted anything because it was a brand, a label or because everyone else had one. I gave him a Tag Heuer watch when he was fifteen or sixteen and I don't think he wore it more than once or twice.

He was honest, sincere in his heart and in his intentions. What you saw with Dominic was what you got. No airs or graces. But he was a humble and polite young man, and at party time he was the life and soul. Without wanting to be the centre of attention, he just was. He loved life, he loved being with his friends or family and made the most of it when he could. He laughed a lot and he swore a lot, which Susan constantly told him off about. I would give my right arm to hear his voice again, even if it was just Anglo Saxon.

We worked closely together over the last two years and my admiration for his knowledge about 'stuff', his work ethic, his capability to absorb extra duties and his ability to know the right thing to do or say at the right time, can't be expressed in a few words. I can only say that not many fathers get to work with their sons, and experience them as adults so closely and so early in their lives. Luckily, I did, and I was so proud to introduce him to people we met during the course of business or pleasure.

'This is Dominic, my son.'

As your children get older you don't notice the slow change in the relationship that you have with them. Eventually, there is some kind of role reversal. Over the last few years, I'd been asking Dominic for his opinion almost every day. Not just about 'stuff', but in the course of our business, there were very few decisions I made without at least listening to his point of view. My pledge to him is that I will try to live my life as he lived: appreciating my friends, my family, the simple things, to try to achieve what makes them and me 'happy'.

Late at night after I locked up at the Sportsmans Inn, Dom and I would stop and chat over a pint. He liked to talk about technology or about gadgets, or about his latest eBay purchase, often something bought for under £5. He liked a bargain but it was always something simple that made his day. Or we would stop on one of the unlit back roads as he was driving back to the Sportsmans from our other pub, the Oddfellows, and I was driving back to Vicargate. He always flashed me first in the dark as he recognised my car headlights.

'Orite, what's the craic?' he would say.

This happened to Susan just a few days before he died. They stopped on the road between Vicargate and the Sportsmans, Eminem emanating from the open window.

She said to him, 'You look happy.'

'I'm loving life at the moment!' he replied.

# A Small Step

Two weeks after Dom's funeral, I started bereavement counselling. I eventually told Colin, my counsellor, I was still going to weekly lectures and I was still writing, despite Dom's death. He told me this was a good thing and creative writing would help me move on in the healing process. I asked him why he thought creativity was a positive thing and how it would help. He didn't know psychologically how it helped; he just knew that it was another tool he had in his grief counselling kit bag. I saw Colin on and off for nine months, but it was that five-minute conversation that put me on a ten-year epic journey of research. In the meantime, he suggested another exercise. He asked me to write a letter to myself pretending it was from Dom. He said that I should imagine his words, his language, to think about his age and what he would say to me about the car crash and his death

That letter is included later on in this book. Colin's suggestion got me thinking, not only about creativity and fiction, but also about what Dom's viewpoint might be on other matters, such as literature, poetry, the landscape, the Lakes and the huge amount of space that he and his friends occupied as they grew up. So, as well as writing the letter from Dom as Colin suggested, I've also added a few comments that he 'might' have said. These are at several points to the right of the page within a few sections of the book. These are also things he 'might' have texted me from his phone, perhaps questioning a decision or a remark I've made.

I still do speak with him about stuff when I go down to his grave, but he never replies even in my head. It's always a monologue but I don't care. How long will it keep him close to me doing it that way?

\*\*\*

Despite Colin's dedication to my survival, I realised that most people are uncomfortable talking about death. Not because they don't care, but out of the fear of the unknown, and the lack of preparedness for death. No-one wants to say the wrong thing, and the death of a real person, a young person, someone they actually know, is uncharted ground. After Dom was killed, I remember walking through Penrith. On at least two occasions, people I know crossed the road to avoid me. I was hurt, but I think it goes part of the way towards explaining why a grief memoir is a growing genre: they create a safe forum, a public space where we can learn to talk safely about death, dying, and grief, without actually coming face to face with it.

I started my diary and the memoir in early 2014. I wrote something every day because I was also studying for my MA. The lines and narrative between the course work and the diary entries quickly blurred. Some fictional pieces I wrote became about Dominic, and even a black teenager protagonist in *One Hundredth*, the novel I was writing, morphed into Dom, adopting his personality traits, his language, style and his philosophy.

Memoir is usually seen as a deeply psychological personal and reflective exploration. I felt that I wasn't just writing about the death of my son and its impact on me: I was also mapping out the narrative arc, the intimate details and emerging silhouettes of this horrific but mysterious thing called grief that so many of us experience. At this point someone had recommended that I read Dr Kübler Ross's *On Death and Dying* (1969) as she identifies the model, the 'Five Stages of Grief'. I did read the book, but it really was more about death and dying as the title suggests, and not about death and grief. It left me wanting. I needed a more in-depth understanding of my despair. I was constantly looking for symbols and metaphors.

# 'No one ever told me that grief felt so much like fear'

One of Dom's favourite movies was the Harold Ramis screenplay Groundhog Day. Grief is like being trapped in Phil Connor's repetitive nightmare. You re-live the same madness and feelings of helplessness and loss every day, and like Phil you can see no escape.

'No one ever told me that grief felt so much like fear' is the first line from CS Lewis's *A Grief Observed* (1960). At the start of my personal journey, this was the first grief memoir recommended to me. In fact, although I didn't realise it at the time, it was the start of the journey of this book. Like Phil, my clock strikes at 6am every morning and I find myself locked into my own 'Groundhog Day', no end in sight to the guilt of not really knowing why, and what Dom was thinking when he got into that car.

## Fade to Black

Grass verges merge with the tarmac at 100 miles an hour. In the dark, on a narrow unlit country lane, when the driver lost control, was Dominic afraid? Did he think he was going to die as the car left the road to plough through a hedge, roll in the air, finally hitting the wall? I've convinced myself that it happened so quickly that he didn't have time. He felt no pain. In those seconds before the blackness, as the car spun through the air and his knuckles turned white, did he call out for anyone? In that millisecond, as the driver turned the steering wheel clockwise to protect himself, and live, did fear turn to hate?

# Fade to White

Lewis's *A Grief Observed* is iconic and has offered solace, respite and insight to grieving readers worldwide for nearly six decades. Lewis wrote then, 'All reality is iconoclastic.' We are all iconolaters – our lives revolve around images, brands and aspiration; it's the new human condition – that is until we lose someone or something important; at that point we leave reality behind. That atom-splitting moment when your tiny world vaporises into a zillion pieces and when you try to collect them, they are lost forever. You will never be whole again. You're sitting in the church, surrounded by the fog, wondering what is real and what isn't.

## Sorrow

People are dressed in black, the hymns are poignant, the words iconic. The church is a beautifully mysterious infrequent stranger, a crucifix the focal point. The moment is sad, so you are sad. But is that the same feeling that we get after finishing an idyllic holiday and getting ready to leave, sorry it has to end? The real pain hasn't even left your brain yet; it's waiting for a trigger. Maybe something as simple as dirty dinner plates in the sink will be the spark?

## Regret

The night air is cooled by a slow pirouetting breeze from the sea. It suddenly rumbas around the balcony as you sip your last local gin and tonic and it gently flirts with your loosely buttoned linen shirt. Through the French doors, your suitcase is open on the bed and is almost packed to go home. A coloured ribbon around the handle – so you can easily spot it on the conveyer belt – stands out against the white sheet. Omniscient soft lighting accentuates the stillness of the pool. Deck chairs are curled up in the shadows. You sigh. 'What a brilliant holiday! You know, I think I could live here.' You take one last long lingering look from the balcony and then set your alarm for an early flight. I'm thinking about when we were all in Mexico together as a family and spent one of our last 'warm' holidays together. Today, I'm not on holiday. I am afraid. I fear the future without Dom. I fear for Dom now without a future, and so I fear what might happen to me at my own hand. At a subterranean level, instinctively, I know that writing is making me think about life. The life Dom has lost, and about ending mine. I just can't make any sense of it, life.

# 3 October 2014

This morning I found the suicide note I'd typed on my iPad last night.
I was drunk, can't remember doing it. But I did. TBH, I can't remember going to bed?
Do I mean it?
I need to write something; Dom died twelve months ago today. Anything…
I Googled the definition of insanity.
It was a start.

# 4 October 2014

Today, slightly more clearheaded, I'm still alive. I didn't think that far ahead a year ago. Taking stock now, emotionally, physically, looking in the mirror; I'm a faint outline, a silhouette of the person I was before 4 October 2013. An empty shell, still trying to understand the reasons why I'm still breathing and he's not? I'm now trying to adjust to living a different life that I can't escape.

I've wished a million times it was me in that car – they say that insanity is doing the same thing over and over again and expecting different results – not just because I want to end the pain of everyday life, but so Dominic can enjoy the rest of his. I've hoped I could go to sleep and not wake up. This would be a simpler outcome all round, not waking up. No questions, not even from the insurance company.

When I do wake up, the first thing in my eyeline is the wooden beam across the vaulted bedroom ceiling, ten feet off the ground, just at the right height to step off Susan's makeup stool. Sometimes when driving on the motorway, I leave my seat belt off on purpose. It would be easy to let go of the steering wheel, close my eyes and put my foot hard down on the accelerator and cross the hard shoulder at 80 mph. I've already picked the optimum spot.

I still drink every day – at times when the urge is bad, anything I can find. The other day, drunk, I wrote that suicide note. A line at the end says:

'If I was so unhappy with my life, would I really be arsed to actually write everything down like this, I'd just do it...' I think about suicide every day, but I'm a coward. I even thought about getting myself certified: this madness is my new normal.

As a way out, committing suicide seems easy. You close your eyes and step into the path of a train or a twenty-ton articulated lorry. Then, of course, you've got a traumatised driver and distressed pedestrians. Should you let this worry you – you'll be dead, spread over fifty yards of railway lines or tarmac?

Yes, I decide, but that's mainly because I am a coward and can't imagine the pain of that initial contact, not because I'm concerned about the wellbeing of my fellow human beings. It won't reverse time. Dominic will still not be leaving that car alive.

There are many different ways to take your own life, albeit some too painful to contemplate, but six thousand people in the UK take their own lives every year, and over forty thousand in the US. Are they more damaged or just braver than me? The perfect storm for suicide seems to be the feeling that your life is pointless and not worth living. You're in the wrong mood at the wrong time; the right opportunity presents itself as there's no-one around to save you. The right tools for the job will make things run more smoothly, and so will having the motivation to go through with it. I seem to have all those boxes ticked. There are now of course suicide bombers who not only take their own lives but those of total strangers; they are motivated by totally different reasons from you when you're thinking about taking your life. This would be quicker, less painful, a suicide vest, but clearly not an option.

Judy, Dominic's grandmother, became very distant over the nine weeks after Dom died, and was found dead in her bed by my daughter, Chloe. The coroner reported excessive amounts of paracetamol in her body. That must have been a very brave thing for her to do, but extremely painful. The physical pain taking over from the heart-breaking pain of losing your grandchild, the pain of your organs slowly closing down, liver and kidneys, stomach pain and finally bleeding from everywhere. I share the emotional pain with her of seeing images of Dominic flash in my head every few minutes. They drive me insane because they just swipe away every other thought, without warning. She will have had those images too, which is perhaps why she decided enough was enough.

I've Googled every possible way of taking my own life. I've decided that suicide would require more courage and strength than I've got at the moment. Paracetamol would be the last resort. I'm writing this because I am still alive, and I'd rather have the memories of Dom, with all the agony they cause, than nothing. Up to this point, I have taken 10,500,000 breaths since Dom was killed. It's him: the thought of him, the essence of him as an individual, the fact that he wouldn't forgive me if I left his mother, brother and sister without a husband and father. It's him at twenty-two years old that would say 'What doesn't kill ya' makes ya' stronger' that keeps me alive, for now. That's one of the 'life' rules that Dom lived by. Dominic hadn't heard of Friedrich Nietzsche, but his philosophy on life, his belief in himself, and his strength through adversity was instinctive.

Dominic was the captain of his soul although not master of his fate as WE Henley wrote in his poem Invictus (Book of Verses, 1888). He was a leader, and you ask yourself whether it was Dom Loftus or Nietzsche that wrote:

> The individual has always had to struggle to keep from being overwhelmed by the tribe. If you try it, you will be lonely often, and sometimes frightened. But no price is too high to pay for the privilege of owning yourself.

Dom was the only person I knew who was comfortable in his own skin, and throughout his life he constantly put other people first. The other thing that keeps me going is a promise after Dominic was killed that I would write a book of memories for him. For his family and his friends to keep all of Dom's life in one place.

## A kind of kindred spirit...

Two things happened on the same day in September 2014 that threatened to change the direction of that. There were two separate conversations with two women who didn't know each other, but each had lost their father, one earlier that year, and one in 2000. I was talking to them because they had contacted me about a piece I'd written in a Cumbrian newspaper. It was early in my grief and I was surprised how they had handled it differently, even from each other. During the conversations I could sense that they had been hurt badly, and felt lost, angry, confused, sad, and lonely, and alive, as they talked about their fathers. They spoke about their loss but also about the things that they took comfort in.

Julie, a journalist, was touched by a statement I'd made to the press following the sentencing on 5 September 2014 of the drunk driver who killed Dominic. The driver pleaded guilty to 'Causing death by careless driving whilst under the influence of alcohol', on the day of the trial. After a discount for pleading guilty, he received five years. Julie understood the part of the process of grief that I had reached, but she was fourteen years ahead of me. She also thought about her own children, putting herself in my shoes. She couldn't contemplate how she would feel if it happened to her. She couldn't imagine standing in the same room as the driver during the trial. She did, however, share something that she had written about her father at the time of his death. It hit home and read:

> 'It is seven months now since my dad died. People still stop me in the street to ask how I am, and tell me how much they miss him. Others, possibly worried about any hysterical outbursts, never mention his death and shuffle awkwardly if I talk about him. Both approaches are fine.
>
> As a grieving person I know I am emotionally vulnerable. Some days are good, some days are very bad. However, I do have a particular objection to the phrase 'you'll get over it'. If someone you love with all your heart dies, you surely never fully recover. I know, in time, whole days will pass when I don't think of my dad. I understand weeks will eventually go by when I don't wake up in the middle of the night hoping he is happy. And I'm sure months will roll on, and the tears will dry. There will, however, never be a time when I stop looking for him in crowds. When I do a double-take at any grey-haired man with glasses who wears a coat like my dad's. I can't ever imagine not wanting to ring him and tell him my good news; to ask him to take my sons to St Bees; to find out how to prune my roses; to moan about the world; to hear that as long as I'm happy, the rest of the world can go to hell. And it'll never cease to break my heart when my oldest son – whose own explanation for his Granda's absence is that 'he's at work' – tells me he's just going to 'put a coat on and go and see Granda Dixon'.
>
> It is difficult to know what to say to grieving people. I've seen bereaved acquaintances in the street and spent a panicked minute

wondering whether to pretend to ignore them or tell them a funny story about their deceased loved one. There is no easy answer. I have discovered I like hearing stories about my dad playing dirty at rugby in his youth and listening to people talk about what he meant to them. People who have lost someone close to them can still laugh at jokes, go on holiday, enjoy episodes of EastEnders and dance to their favourite music. This is not 'getting over' death; this is 'getting on' with life. There is a difference.' (Julie, September 2014).

\*\*\*

I started to recognise that what Julie told me about her reaction to her father's death is similar to mine. The feeling of inconsolable emptiness, the gap that he has left in her heart cannot be filled with extra love for other people in our lives. It's his gap, and no-one else's. I can take a great deal of comfort from her. Julie has written to me several times; she is a well-balanced, intelligent, if not a 'cocky' (her words) individual. The 'madness' – the times I think I'm losing the plot – is normal. That one conversation has helped so much. She described the same sense of confusion and the need to understand all the 'whys' that I'm going through, and her understanding is that it's all part of the process. She has lived through fourteen years of grief with dignity, and she knows that grief is unforgiving. In a brief moment of normality, a moment of pride, for example, watching Reuben, Dominic's younger brother, score a try for Penrith Rugby team, grief slaps me in the face; it's a reminder that it's still here and that Dominic isn't.

I now try to see or imagine Dom in the Lake District, his place of birth and one of the greatest gifts, as parents, we were able to give him. Whilst I can draw comfort in his love for the fells and countryside, at the same time it's painful that he's not here to enjoy it. It's a beautiful place to live and a mecca for poets and artists. As a romantic writer, I want to imagine that it was where his heart was too, and that he still walks the fells with Lucy. In reality – and as the father of a dead son – I have investigated and googled every known culture and their views on the afterlife, but know he lies at St Kentigern's Church, buried deep in the ancient soil of Castle Sowerby. However, I question if this is how other writers see their loved ones, finally located in a quiescent and safe, happy place? Helen MacDonald does this in *H is For Hawk* when the narrative goes back to when she was a child, and to the happy memories she shared with her father of training small hawks. Her happy, quiet place.

    The other thing that happened was that Jane, the other woman I've known for a long time, also spoke about her dad, and she felt a similar loss to Julie but took a different view about the future and was more reflective about her dad's life. She said her dad's church service was a small one, but the vicar was very thoughtful and talked about the 'dash' on memorials or in obituaries. It took a while to work that out, but what she meant was the dash between people's birthday and the date of their death. Dominic's stone says, 16 January 1991 – 4 October 2013. His dash represents twenty-two years and ten months. Jane's father's 'dash' was nearly eighty years and he was ill; she sat with him as he died and said goodbye. Dominic's 'dash' is less than twenty-three years and he died instantly and unexpectedly. His adult life had just started and I didn't get the chance to say goodbye. This is the ultimate pain, like Julie's, that no-one wants to imagine happening to them.

    Jane's view is that her dad, whilst she misses him terribly, had a good and long life. So, does she feel a different pain or grief from Julie and me? A less intense loss? Or is it the way she has decided to view his death? Still, she misses him every day, and the hole in her heart is 'Dad' shaped as much as mine is 'Dom' shaped. Both of these women helped me in different ways. I Googled *The Dash* which is a poem by Linda Ellis (1996) and is in Appendix 4. It added another missing piece into the grief jigsaw.

***

Sometimes it's a lonely journey; despite your public smile no-one understands or knows what's going on in your head or behind closed doors. Occasionally you see light at the end of the tunnel and pray it's not a train coming the other way. Mostly in the beginning you hope it is. Yesterday, an ex-soldier and author told me about the death of his brother. 'It's like losing an arm; eventually you learn to adapt your life to being mono-dexterous, and you get on with it. Sometimes, and in certain situations, you do think that it would be really good to have your other arm back.'

A full year after Dom's death, I haven't grown another arm, but I have grown another face. I am destined for the foreseeable future to be facing in two directions, looking back to the past with my sad face and to the future with my 'public' face, like a politician's permanent perfunctory smile. Janus, the omniscient Roman God, also has two faces, one facing to the past and one facing to the future. Is that my punishment? In grief we are Janus; we are the God with two faces. As humans and not Gods, can we do both at the same time without ripping ourselves apart? Whilst Janus was the God with many faces, to the Romans he was the most important God, the God of beginnings, of gates, transitions, time, duality, doorways, passages and ending. Dom, too, had many faces: the hard-working professional, the fast-living party animal, and of course, when he wanted to drop off the grid with his farming friends, the straw-chewing country bumkin.

Janus was also the transitional gate between war and peace, therefore between life and death. Even before Dom's death I believed that if, as individuals, we make the right decisions and go through the right doors we are in control over our own lives. Janus represents the view that symbolically you are in charge of your own destiny. When you read about the Roman Gods at school, Janus is positioned simply as the god of doors; however, once you start to examine him in more depth his perceived responsibility as 'concierge' changes dramatically. He had a profound and deep influence on Roman society, culture and its value system.

I have tried desperately to understand or come to some sort of philosophical position on the meaning of this journey with Dom, researching current cultures and historical societies like that of the Romans, exploring and opening as many literary and virtual doors as possible. I've read critical thinkers from Orwell – 'The best books… are those that tell you what you know already' (1984) – to Nietzsche – 'To live is to suffer, to survive is to find some meaning in the suffering' (*On the Genealogy of Morality*). What does Nietzsche mean about meaning? In order to continue to do this, I have to strip out the abstract and examine the concrete elements first: the birth, the struggle and then the death. Life is about travelling through gates and doors, and the choices that we make. It seems brutal, almost dismissive, to write it down like that, but for the last year I've knocked on doors, stopped time, fallen down traps, gone up blind alleyways and travelled deep into dark rabbit holes. I've faced many transitions through my reading and writing whilst looking for meaning. I miss Dominic – that hasn't changed because I'm looking for answers – but how do I open the next door?

Inevitably, like many bereaved writers before me, I now find myself asking if God and religion are a crutch, a convenient way to abandon our responsibility of finding, opening and closing the doors of our own lives and shaping their direction? This is a journey towards the understanding and the meaning of life or death. For some people it might be to find and worship a god, but for others, it's to realise that they are their own deity and destiny. At some stage we discover that we are monotheistic and you actually believe in yourself and in your own ability to influence your own life.

Ludwig Feuerbach (1804–1872), philosopher, atheist and major influence on Karl Marx, wrote in his book *The Essence of Christianity* (1841), 'the turning point of history will be the moment man becomes aware that the only God of man is man himself'. When Marx was asked what his objective in life was, he said, 'To dethrone God and destroy capitalism!' When everything was denounced including the scriptures, morals, immortality, the existence of the spirit and the sanctity of individual human life, the dialectical materialists such as Feuerbach, Marx and Engels interestingly turned to the worship of themselves. In my view, there is a point in your grief and your recovery when self-belief becomes more important than a belief in God. It is not a replacement but a search for inner strength. The materialists also state that self-preservation is the supreme instinct in man, and that is where I find myself now. How do I survive?

I have always respected friends' views and religious beliefs, and respected the church for its general pastoral care, but I have never been a believer of an omniscient being who created life and the earth in a few days. However, I do believe in a sincere young man who promoted love in a hostile world, who encouraged friendship and understanding in a war of cultures, and I believe sincerely he was nailed to a cross for his beliefs.

So why do we default to God in times of crisis? Either asking him to help us out of the problem, or usually, blaming him for not helping us and getting us into the crisis in the first place. 'If there is a God, why did he let this happen?'

# Early Influences – Gods, Caesar and Mungo

The Romans had no direct influence on Dom, but they had a huge impact on the Lake District, and the Lakes shaped Dom. The Scottish Border region was the frontier of their empire. Although Hadrian's Wall wasn't built until 120 AD, Caesar came here twice, in 55 BC and 54 BC. Dominic lived most of his life surrounded by Roman artefacts, forts and fortlets from Ambleside to Wigton – sunken dwellings in the shadow of the Northern Massif, the range of fells north of Keswick. These mountains, often snow-covered for four or five months of the year, start at Blencathra, end at High Pike, then drop down into the village of Caldbeck. At its centre is the Oddfellows Arms, a pub, restaurant and small hotel that we bought in 2011. For the two years leading up to his death, Dominic worked there, and we had rooms set aside for him when he was cooking and pulling pints.

Caldbeck is a grey-stoned, rugged, traditional Lakeland village, where little has been touched or changed by the wider world for centuries. There is no mobile signal, but there are unsmiling, impenetrable people who have their own nuances of tradition and values. People from the outside fail to understand this micro, introverted society. Consequently, they fail to integrate within it and subsequently they are always incomers of the village. Even though Dominic was born and bred a Cumbrian lad, he struggled with the parochial and insular way of life many of the indigenous people led.

The Cumbrian countryside is a vast area where large extended families dominate. Land and farms have been handed down to the eldest son over generations, and some acquired by 'other' means over the years. Many of these families were deeply divided by foot and mouth disease, and still are. Many others became millionaires overnight because of it.

Just recently in the village, two men, one aged forty-two and the other fifty-five years old, were caught out 'tupping' a couple of young girls. The younger is eighteen, and the other is twenty-two years old. It's an age-old story, older men getting together with young girls; it happens all around the world. The age difference in Caldbeck is more glaring and bordering on paedophilia. The village is a small tightknit area of eight or nine hundred residents, and, when they don't let incomers in easily, it's a very shallow gene pool.

Dominic said to me one day after a particularly hard shift at The Oddfellows:

'You know, Dad, every village has an idiot, a busybody, a pisshead, a know it all, a serial shagger and a prick who drives a BMW. Sometimes two or three of these characters are actually the same person.'

I didn't know it at the time, but he was talking about the driver of the car that killed him.

\*\*\*

Dom started his journey and early education at Caldbeck, attending Fellview Primary School, leaving to go south to Penrith as soon as we could take him. He realised even at eleven years old that he needed brighter lights and more enlightened friends.

This narrative journey with Dom, however, isn't about death; it's about love.

> *but you hardly ever told me that you loved me I know you did when i was a kid ;-) haha i was on top of the world when you carried me on your shoulders and i wished my mates could have seen you and me sat on the ride on mower cutting the grass even if i did fall asleep but when I was fourteen, we used to argue in the car about what i was doing at school I thought that you didn't even like me*

Apart from his family and cars, Dom's great love was the Cumbrian landscape. From an early age, he explored the fells, the forgotten paths and bridleways on a quad-bike, then a scrambling bike, then a 4X4. Eighteen months before his death, it was often on foot with Lucy, his border collie. This was more than a pastime; even whilst working he preferred driving on country roads rather than the main roads.

The Lake District also has been a county that attracts poets, painters, writers and homegrown fox hunters that have songs written about them. For example, 'D'ye Ken John Peel?', about John Peel, a famous eighteenth-century Cumbrian huntsman. Like Dominic, Peel was from the Caldbeck area, a likeable rogue and a man prone to dissipation. His friend and neighbour John Woodcock Graves (1795–1886) wrote the lyrics to the song in the Cumbrian dialect, and set them to the tune of a traditional Scottish song, called 'Bonnie Annie'. Like Peel, Dominic also had poems and songs written about him. Graves travelled to Tasmania from Caldbeck, where he lived out the rest of his life. I have the only remaining oil painting of him, but our paths cross on a personal matter. His eldest son John, a successful barrister, died as Dom did, before his father. I feel Graves's pain almost one and a half centuries later; I can see it in his portrait's eyes.

The other thing that John Peel and Dominic have in common is that they are both buried in St Kentigern's church, Peel in Caldbeck and Dom in Castle Sowerby, the parishes where they were born. Sadly, both of them have had their graves vandalised. Peels was damaged by anti-hunt protesters, one hundred and fifty years after his death, and Dom's by an unknown assailant between 4–6 May 2015, eighteen months after his death.

*FFS dad you no as well as I do who did it…*

As is the Christian tradition, Dom's grave faces to the east, so the Northern Massif landscape is behind him. He hasn't turned his back on his beloved hills; in fact just the opposite: his grave basks in the sunrise from the east above Penrith and falls into shadow as the sun sets on the other side of High Pike and Caldbeck. It's a passage of the sun he knows well, growing up at Vicargate, two fields away from his grave. The church was founded in the sixth century by St Kentigern, or Mungo, as he was also known. He had a major influence on large areas of Cumbria, digging wells to baptise the hill dwellers and building several churches on his missionary journey from Scotland to Wales. Legend has it that Kentigern converted Merlin (Myrddin) to Christianity during his time in the Scottish Borders, as depicted in the stained-glass window in a church in Tweeddale.

One of Dom's favourite places to visit was Bowscale Tarn, near an isolated hamlet named after St Mungo, nestled between Mosedale and Mungrisdale.

As a man, he was often up there with Lucy.
As a teenager, Dom worked at the Mill Inn, the only pub in Mungrisdale.

The tarn is a dark, brooding place. It's 56 feet deep, but to Dom, it was an oasis of solitude and serenity. As mentioned earlier, according to folklore, two immortal fish live in the tarn and it's these fish that appear in Wordsworth's 1888 poem 'Song at the Feast of Brougham Castle'.

Dom would mention the tarn in his texts and take pictures of Lucy on his phone fetching the sticks and tennis balls that he'd thrown into the enigmatic water.

*there u go agen*
*i don't even no who this wordsworth gadg is*
*but ur right tho its the best place*
*lucy loved the water*

According to Cumbrian legend, Mungo's mother was a princess, the daughter of King Lleuddun who ruled the lands of Lothian in Scotland. She became pregnant after being raped by the son of Urien, the King of Rheged (c.590). In a twisted act of early medieval honour killing, her father had her thrown off

Traprain Law, a hill in east Lothian. She survived the fall and made her way across the River Forth to Fife. Mungo was born and brought up by St Serf, who was ministering to the Picts. It was Serf who gave him his name, Mungo, which means 'Dear Friend'. An anti-Christian movement in Strathclyde made it difficult for Mungo and he left the area and travelled to Wales, via Cumbria.

After a pilgrimage to Rome, he returned to Glasgow, where a large community grew up around him. In old age, it is said that Mungo became very weak and was so feeble that his chin had to be kept in place with a bandage. He died in his bath.

# 28 July 2014, 10.38 am

'Ian?'

'Hello, William. How are you?' Nervously.

'Bad news, I'm afraid. It's Mum.'

My mother had gone to the bathroom at 6 am that morning and never came out alive. Whilst she wasn't ill, she wasn't a fit or well woman. I knew she was dead. It was the phone call. My brother William never rang, and it was his choice of those first two words. I'm numb, but how can I grieve any more than I am? I have nothing left inside, all sensation has gone and there is nothing unexpended left to offer. The last time I saw her she was really sad and deeply regretted that she couldn't go to Dominic's funeral. She was in hospital recovering from an operation. During my last visit I played the YouTube video of Reuben singing in the church. We all cried together.

I drove to Penrith after William's call, thinking about that last visit I'd made to see my mother. Hindsight. We do that when we grieve. We wish that we could see into the future, and we say, 'If only I'd known that would be the last time.' The gears in the car change themselves. I was on auto-pilot, numb, not knowing what to think or even how or what I should feel. I loved my Mum but felt nothing as the forest flashed by on either side of the narrow road, the canopy hiding any sun. Before I knew it, I'd driven seven miles and had stopped at the T-junction that led into the first village after Vicargate and the entrance to Greystoke Castle. The cover of the trees had broken and the sun tried to penetrate the traffic film on my windscreen. It couldn't, but the sound of well-shod hooves did. In single file, a dozen race horses from the Nicky Richard's stable slowly and majestically turned into the village. The jockeys high above me all gave the thumbs up for slowing down and stopping. I raised a hand to acknowledge their presence and looked into their faces. They smiled. They didn't know my mother had just died. I recognised a face in the middle of the pack. He was a good friend and he knew Dom. He didn't smile but he nodded once in my direction and looked ahead again. I must remember to tell him about my mother, I thought.

As I drove out of the other side of Greystoke, back on auto-pilot, a small stoat ran across the road in front of me. I looked at the rear-view mirror and it was motionless in my tyre track, dead. I had to pull over. Was it anger or frustration that tore into me? I'd just killed something; I'd ended a life, instantly. Then, regret. Why me? Why now? Why didn't I leave the house earlier or later? Why didn't the stoat just wait five more seconds? There can't be a God. God wouldn't have allowed me to kill an innocent animal. And then guilt and sorrow as I sobbed uncontrollably in the lay-by. Was it for the stoat, my mum or for Dom? Or was it for me?

***

Although he knew and loved the Cumbrian landscape, Dom rarely talked about or engaged with its history or the fantastical Cumbrian legends on which the county is based. So perhaps it's ironic that he's buried in a place so rich in legend. Castle Sowerby, located between Greystoke and Caldbeck, is one of the eight churches dedicated to St Kentigern in the diocese of Carlisle. Dom is now permanently intertwined and resident in one of them, forever linked to Mungo and John Peel. I found a verse that was written about the four miracles it's said that Mungo performed. It encapsulates my guilt about what Dom lost, and metaphorically, the things that he never experienced.

Here is the bird that never flew
Here is the tree that never grew
Here is the bell that never rang
Here is the fish that never swam

Like most young teenagers, Dom liked playing war games on his games console, not realising that his own birthplace had always been fought over by invading armies. These invasions go further back than St Mungo and his decision to convert us to Christianity in the sixth century. Thankfully, the only invasions we've encountered over the last three hundred years have been for the sake of art and education. Apart from the mounting tourism over the last few centuries, they were subtle, slow and usually involved armies of writers, artists and tourists. They made pilgrimages to the Lakes for the same reasons that the Picts did from the north, the Romans from the south and the Norse, who invaded from the east: the richness of the place. Many of the artists finally settled here and are not Cumbrian by birth. They've taken its people, the haunting glacial atmosphere and its history and adopted it into their hearts and made it their own, and consequently made it famous.

*yeah but theyll never be cumbrian just like you*
*dad even after 41 years*
*they hate incomers you no that*

# Seventeen

In the mid-eighteenth century, the opportunity of travelling for enjoyment was not common and only for the rich, but developments in rail infrastructure soon opened up tourism to the wider population. Prior to this, travel for pleasure and personal development was for those wealthy enough to finance the Grand Tour – a cultural route through northern Europe which served as a rite of passage for the British nobility and the wealthy. It was designed to educate and enrich the aristocratic mind. At seventeen, Dominic's Grand Tour, his rite of passage, wasn't as grand as those of, say, Beckford, Shelley or Byron, who took inspiration from Rome, Athens and Florence, but to most of his farming friends who have never left the parish, he may as well have gone to the moon. In 2008, he undertook his own journey of liberal education, cultural stimulation and self-discovery in Lanzarote, one of the Canary Islands. While there, he also learned how to drink a lot.

I was also seventeen when I left home to work at a holiday camp in Pwllheli North Wales. It was 1976, one of the hottest UK summers on record. I think of those halcyon days and hope that the experience Dom had in the Grand Canaries was similar to mine. I was free, and even in that Welsh summer heat I worked and played hard. There is an innocence at that age, a carefree naivety that I saw in Dom too. As Grand Tourists, our journeys opened up our minds, an enlightenment that we shared at the same age. We both had little or no responsibility and no bills to pay. The money we earned was ours to spend on our journey of discovery, and this freedom offered us the opportunity to learn and to do new things not available at home. Dom loved the University of Lanzarote and graduated with a first in life. He returned to Vicargate and Cumbria as an established legend, well, in Castle Sowerby at least. From there, he continued his exploration of the Lakes, the landscape and himself.

The Cumbrian landscape has always had this impact on people. The Romantic poets of the late-eighteenth and nineteenth centuries, such as William Wordsworth, Samuel Coleridge, Thomas de Quincey and John Ruskin, were greatly moved by the place. It infected the work of modern writers such as Melvyn Bragg, who was born less than seven miles from where Dom ran the pub at Caldbeck. Children's authors also have drawn inspiration from the landscape, such as Beatrix Potter, Arthur Ransome of *Swallows and Amazons* fame and John Cunliffe, the creator of *Postman Pat*. Another influential writer of the Lake District landscape was Alfred Wainwright, the author of many walking guides to the area. Most of these guides overlap areas of the fells that overflow with fantastical ancient folklore: marching ghost armies, talking fish, vampires, forest-dwelling outlaws, legendary kings with round tables, noble knights from Inglewood Forest, and wizards. Dom didn't read Wainwright's books and guides, but he will have unknowingly walked many of the routes that Wainwright explored, drew and painstakingly detailed for us.

These reckless, adventurous and sometimes naïve young men are the bedrock of Cumbrian folklore. Their stories remind me of Dom and his friends. Take the legend of the Cumbrian outlaw, Adam Bell, renamed and reinvented as the Robin Hood of the Midlands. Dominic and his friends spent all their summers, spare time and weekends in the woods near Heggle Lane and the fields and fells in the surrounding area. They reminded me of Bell's medieval story and his band of brothers, camping in clearings, cooking over open fires and drinking booze, 'liberated' from parents.

The poem 'Adam Bell', printed by Wynkyn de Worde in 1505, captures this male camaraderie:

> Mery it was in the grene forest
> Among the leves grene
> Where that man walke both east and west
> Wyth bowes and arrowes kene

Dom and the boys had air rifles and shotguns and spent their time hunting rabbit, hare and crow. I'm not sure if Dom and his merry mates actually shot much or cooked any of it, but there was certainly lots of fun, bonding and merriment in the forest. I still have Dom's rifle. On the day we were moving from the Sportsmans to Newbiggin, I removed it from its soft sheepskin sheath to clean it. I remember setting up the sights with him when he was about sixteen. Later, we took turns shooting cans off the gazebo wall. He was so happy that day. The gun was one of his first grown up purchases.

Adam Bell and his two Merry Men, William of Cloudsley and Clym the Clough, were living in the woods near Unthank, five minutes by crow from Vicargate, and were caught stealing game in the Forest of Inglewood. This is still an estate today, north of Penrith. The current Lord Inglewood, Richard, resides there but the house has been opened up to the public and Richard spent many years as an MEP.

As the legend goes, Bell and his boys were made outlaws by the then Lord of the manor. After escaping to Carlisle, about fifteen miles away, the three men were captured. The King agreed to pardon Adam and the Merry Men if Adam could shoot an apple placed on his young son's head at a distance of 120 paces. That sounds like a familiar story too. Adam, a master longbow man, did just this and earned his pardon. I joked with Dom about putting an empty coke can on Reuben's head to test the sights on his gun, but he just gave me that, 'You're an idiot' look, but with a twinkle in his eye.

\*\*\*

If Dominic had been born around the time of the tourist expansion in the Lakes from 1750 onwards, I fancy his fame would have rivalled that of Mary Robinson, the beautiful daughter of the landlord who ran the pub at Buttermere. In Mary's time, as today, the Lake District had become the place to escape to, offering art tourism for writers, painters and poets who were drawn by its magic, mystery and history. The early pioneers of domestic tourism soon followed and tourism guides flourished. One of the first important guides, *A Fortnight's Ramble in the Lakes in Westmorland, Lancashire and Cumberland,* was written by Joseph Palmer, and appeared in 1792. Among his travel tales and suggested itineraries, Palmer mentioned a beautiful inn keeper's daughter from a village near Keswick:

On our going into it the girl flew away as swift as a mountain sheep, and it was not till our return from Scale Force that we could say that we first saw her. She brought in part of our dinner and seemed to be about fifteen. Her hair was thick and long, of a dark brown, and though unadorned with ringlets did not seem to want them; her face was a fine oval, with full eyes, and lips as red as vermillion, her cheeks had more of the lily than the rose.

This beautiful girl described by Palmer is Mary. She was only fifteen when the book was published. She quickly became famous as the 'Maid of Buttermere'. Like Mary, Dominic was good looking, tall, with classical facial features inherited from his mother. I could envisage Palmer stopping to write about the Oddfellows at Caldbeck or our other pub, the Sportsmans Inn, near Troutbeck, where Dom lived and worked too. Palmer would have been captivated by Dominic's high cheek bones and porcelain skin, 'more of a lily than a rose', his blue eyes, blond hair and his constant smile.

Just like Mary, Dom could be seen pouring pints of real ale for tourists wanting to taste the Cumbrian nectar. Later, laughing with the locals and telling them one of his anecdotes, he would soon become another of Palmer's attractions, slotted in between the Lake's famous viewing-stations and the picturesque landscapes.

'Without contamination doth she live' was one of Wordsworth's descriptions of Mary in *Book VII of The Prelude*, and I could write this about my son too, quite seriously and soberly. Wordsworth's description reveals why Mary became so famous among the Romantic Movement and the tourists to the Lake District. The 'artless daughter of the hills' represented a woman shaped by nature, living 'without contamination' in the 'spot where she was born and reared'. She is 'unspoiled', a product of the natural environment, free from artificial influence, 'in cruel mockery/ of love and marriage bonds'.

In his prelude, Wordsworth might have been describing exactly how Dom and his friends grew up, just as Mary did, unspoiled, off the beaten track, and in the Lake District Northern Fells, their minds and hearts untainted by heaving cities overrun with crime and poverty and where people eat from food banks. Like Mary, Dom and his friends were almost feral, unaffected by domestic or foreign politics or policies. The grass needed to be cut, the sheep still had to be bred, fed and sheared, and the cows needed to be milked and calved. Two hundred years ago the English Romantic poets' preoccupation with nature was one of the driving forces behind the success of Lake District tourism. Today, these boys still keep its equilibrium by living off it, still in tune with nature's basket, but still being free to follow the Cumbrian ghosts like Dom, or Adam Bell, through the seventy-acre woods at Heggle Lane.

In my proud, biased, but humble fatherly opinion, Dom is now added to that long list of Cumbrian legends, myths and mysteries. He was certainly a legend with his friends and customers. My Facebook messenger account is full of stories I received after his death of his kindness and endearing charm. There is one from a young girl who said she could have been a scientist if she hadn't bunked off school lessons with Dom. Is it a myth that he invented the Guinness Bomb: a heady cocktail of Baileys Irish cream and a pint of Guinness? Hundreds of people shared their stories and memories of him after he died. As they sat in pews at the funeral, they created their own memories on cards that Susan had left for them to write on. Many said how thoughtful, sensible and polite Dom was. Yet, it still remains a mystery to me. If he was a wise young man, why did he get into that car on that wet October night?

> *your so full of shit sometimes dad and always try to make things sound better than they are im a normal lad but my mates did think i was a legend tho, ask joe taylor lol*

\*\*\*

I went to see Dominic twice in the chapel of rest. We went as a family on Tuesday, 15 October 2013, and I went on my own on Thursday the 17th, the day before his interment. It's a cliché, but he really did look like he was asleep. I wanted to shake him and wake him up. I touched his chest but he was cold. I had written him a note and slipped it into his pocket. I had my final face to face chat with him. I promised him that I would be strong the next day. I knew a lot of people and many of his young friends would be at the funeral and at his wake and some of them would need support.

I didn't cry on 18 October. None of us did. I didn't even get drunk. I'm not ashamed to say, I've cried almost every day since. The tears are not for my loss; they are for Dominic's loss: his life, his future and his opportunities. I'm pleased I wrote him that final letter; there were two others in his pocket. I didn't look at them because they were private, but I did touch them because they must have been written by someone who cared as much as I did.

*I no who put them there I bet you cant guess who?*

Later, after I'd visited him. I sat in my car at the petrol forecourt crying. I wished I'd had more time and written more thoughts to him. Someone honked their horn behind me to move on and I screamed, 'Don't you know my son's fucking dead?'

She didn't hear me. I moved my car slowly forward. She didn't know, or care, about Dominic. She just needed petrol and a pint of milk.

Often when I'm walking down the street, I seethe and bite my lip with anger at people carrying on their normal lives. I'm mostly angry with young men who don't seem to grasp or understand life. They have no respect as their loud conversations always include the 'F' word in every sentence. They spit on the ground and smoke 'roll-ups' in their white track suit bottoms and Adidas trainers. I'm incensed when I see them and I think,

'Why Dominic? Why not that piece of shit?'

\*\*\*

My Dear Dom,

This is it, 17 October 2013; after tomorrow we won't see you again. We will come to the place where you'll spend the rest of eternity and speak with you there.

I hope you enjoyed the time you had; I know 22 years is less than most people get, but I guess you crammed more in it than most people anyway.

Thank you for being you. I am so proud of you, not just for being my son, but for the man that you turned out to be. You are the best son, workmate and friend a man could ever wish to have.

The gap you have left in our lives is immeasurable and sometimes I don't know how I can continue without you. This isn't what you want to hear, I know. I also know that if you were here, next to me, and you always will be, you'd just smile that huge smile and say, 'You've got to, Ian.'

The picture of you and the Glendale is fantastic and says it all. At the moment, it breaks my heart every time I look at it, because it's just you and how I shall always remember you. In time I hope I can smile instead of cry when I look at it and think of you with happy thoughts.

This isn't a goodbye; it's only some thoughts that I wanted to share with you before the coffin lid closed. There will never be a goodbye in my heart until it finally stops.

You are a good man, Dominic, and lots of people will also miss you terribly. I hope that is proof that the way you have lived your life as you did, is the right way.

I take great comfort that you know how much we love you and care about you, that you died without pain.

Ian

*\*\**

The life that existed before Dom was killed has switched off. Literally. The telephone, TV, radio, CD and DVD players, the internet. The family business is only operating because of a few dedicated people. Dom's light has been extinguished and my life fades to black as the power source to my existence has been flicked off too. What's left? Drinking, writing?

Chloe Lydon, one of those dedicated people from the Sportsmans asked me to email her some documents that she hasn't got access to. Reluctantly, I powered up my laptop and reconnected to the Wi-Fi. Hundreds of emails flooded in. Many of them responding to an interview I did with a newspaper. I didn't recognise many of the names. I opened the first unread message.

## 7 December 2013, at 14:57 (email)

Dear Ian,

I didn't know your son, so can't share any memories with you, but I share you and your wife's pain.

When my daughter Helen Jones was killed in the London Bombing, I was afraid of forgetting things that happened in her life, so I asked all her friends to share their memories as you have done. The book that was produced was purely a private affair for her friends and family and those who win the bursary that was set up in her name.

If it would help, I would be very willing to either send you a copy so that you could see one way of setting it out or if you would like we would be very happy to come down and meet you and give you a copy personally.

Liz.

## 10 December 2013

I, too, am afraid of forgetting things about Dominic. Whilst my head is constantly bombarded with his image, when I actually try to recall a specific memory, I have to work hard to see it clearly. I email Liz and arrange a meeting after Christmas.

## 15 January 2014, The Letter from Dominic

Sorry, Dad, I didn't mean this to happen. It was so sudden I'd even left the TV on. I know that isn't probably much comfort but I did intend to come back that night.

There's nothing more I can do for you now. All the jobs I liked to do around the pubs will have to be done by someone else. The Hellons are good lads; they'll help with all the electrical stuff. I'm sure Ollie and the lads will help you at Vicargate if they can. Simon will step up to the mark at the Sportsmans (one of our businesses) and help Chris (Head Chef). You're going to have to brush up on your DIY skills though. The personal, family, son and Dad stuff, that's where it's really going to hurt; we can't have a drink together at the end of the night on table 19, like we used to, no more meeting on the back roads late at night and having a craic. No more phone calls, no more text messages, no more messages on the new iPhone.

You are probably grieving more about the future than the past, but the memories are the same: the past will always be the past even if I was here now; it's our future that has stopped. There are lots of things that will pass us both by; and that's a big hurt for me, and I guess for you.

No grandchildren; I know that will hurt you more than me, but you know how I feel about kids running around the bar!!!

No more Christmases, no more big piss-ups or parties at Vicargate, no more happy family get-togethers and BBQs in the garden.

No more skiing holidays.

I know I was the first-born and always remember that story you tell everyone about you, Mam and me leaving the hospital when you first took me home. I was in the back of the car in my child seat; you looked at Mam and said, 'You do realise we've got a baby in the back of the car? What do we do now?'

Please don't regret any decisions you may or may not have made. I was a man, and I too made decisions that you had no control of, or perhaps sometimes you didn't know about. Yes, we did talk every day and make decisions together about the business, but I had my own life, Dad, and don't forget I left home when I was 17.

I have no more pain, which is good, but I have no more dreams, just like you, for me.

Will we see each other again? I can't answer that question; I am dead, and just a memory in your head. I know it's powerful and painful at the moment. I know you cry for me every day and not for you, but I understand that you miss me. You have to go on; I will live forever now in your thoughts and I will never grow old. I will always look the same in the pictures and the videos. I will forever be standing in front of the Glendale, with a beer; I will forever have Lucy on my knee, together on the leather chair, me smiling.

I would like to say that the pain is over quickly, but only you will ever know.

Dom

***

In reality, Dom didn't write much, but like most young men, he loved technology and the things that have sprung from it that they take for granted: texting, movies on demand, Bluetooth, and Facebook. For me, social media is a double-edged sword. I'm not interested in what my friend's dog had for breakfast, even if it was the cat, but on what would have been Dom's twenty third birthday, I put the following on Facebook. I wanted people to know that he was still among us, and we were all still his friends on Facebook.

# Today is the day of Dominic's birth, 16th January 1991

It seems appropriate to celebrate and remember his life on the day that we first met him.

He will be forever in our hearts and minds and we will always remember the many Dominics that passed through our lives:

The bundle who came home that week in January; we didn't know what to do with it.

The boy who sat for a cuddle on my knee, sat on our bed talking after coming home late at night, until he was twenty.

The 16-year-old with the yellow 'ped'; his helmet is still in the garden shed.

The young man who packed his rucksack for his first day at work and proudly took a picture of it.

The school boy who fiercely protected his sister when she went to school and argued like cat and dog at home.

The 11-year-old who only played rugby and guitar because he thought I wanted him to.

The baby who walked at ten months.

The Cumbrian lad, up Bowscale Tarn with his collie.

The 12-year-old who got his brand-new phone stolen at school; my heart broke.

The nervous teen who spread his wings, early.

The grumpy teen who spent Saturday mornings on the dry ski slope.

The 2- to 7-year-old who sat on my knee driving the car down the drive.

The 22-year-old competent electrician, barman and chef, who only had three books, all of them about teaching dog tricks.

The man who taught me many of life's lessons.

These are only some of our many Dominics. You will have your own; please share them here, or pass on to someone who you think will have their own Dominic to celebrate today.'

FB 16/01/14. I'm sure his response would be –

> *God dad it took me yonks gettin u online and look at u now – fb!!!!*

# H e l e n

Dominic would get the school bus to Penrith every day until he bought a scooter when he was seventeen, a bright yellow one. We knew he got on the bus, but weren't sure that he actually got to school, or if he did, how long he stayed there. He was a likeable rascal, a Cumbrian Lad, a heart throb and a very hard worker, but he hated school.

Living in rural isolation as we do, getting on the bus was a big adventure for kids like Dominic. The bus would stop at most villages between Vicargate and school, and children would be waiting on crossroads, in the dark, the rain and the snow, depending on the time of year. Consequently, the first hour of every day (that's how long it took to drive the twelve miles to Penrith) was very productive: 'the craic' or homework, 'gentle' banter with the bus driver, or just catching up with sleep. After he got his scooter, he hardly used school or indeed public transport at all. The last time he did was in March 2012 when the whole family, including Linzi, Dom's girlfriend, and Jordan, Chloe's boyfriend, went to New Hampshire for our annual ski trip. We took the train down from Penrith to Euston station, a tube to King's Cross, then of course the Piccadilly line to Heathrow airport for a flight to Boston.

Dominic was twenty-one. He was now a responsible young adult – sensible, a new word added to his vocabulary from the school bus days. I'd hired two fully loaded Cherokee Jeeps to take us from the airport and up into the mountains of New England. I drove one; he drove the other. I was bursting with pride when we arrived at the snowbound hotel 300 miles later, on the wrong side of the road; my likeable rascal, my Cumbrian Lad, was becoming a worldly-wise man. He was hacked off, though. Despite being twenty-one he still had to carry his passport with him. Every bar and restaurant asked for his ID.

Seven years earlier in July 2005, at 8.50 am on 7 July, another young responsible adult, a young woman called Helen, also travelled on a southbound tube on the Piccadilly line. At Russell Square, the unforgettable and the unforgivable happened. Germaine Maurice Lindsay (23 September 1985–7 July 2005), also known as Abdullah Shaheed Jamal, was one of four Islamist terrorists who detonated bombs on three trains on the London Underground and a bus in central London. In total, they killed fifty-six people (including themselves), and injured more than seven hundred. Lindsay detonated the bomb that killed him, Helen and the twenty-five others who were travelling on Helen's train.

Thinking of that moment, of Helen, my thoughts today are sober and sombre. My life seems to have been in a permanent state of undress, going nowhere, like a groom chained to a lamp post on his stag night. My thoughts, erratic, but naked too presented on these pages before you; I can't even begin to imagine what Lindsay was thinking, to take his own life, but Helen's too? What was Helen thinking at 8.50 am on 7 July, before the bomb ripped her body and her train apart? Was it of her Mum?

# 23 February 2014, 2.30 pm, Eden Valley Hospice

Susan didn't want to go; she wasn't ready to meet anyone yet that she didn't know.

'Hi, I'm Ian. I've come to meet Liz.'

The receptionist smiled, nodded and pointed to a woman in a sitting area on the left four or five yards away. I signed the visitors' book as she walked to meet me.

The first time you see someone is the hardest; the time and place are irrelevant. As soon as you hear 'I'm really sorry about Dom; he was a lovely lad' or 'I didn't know him but it must be awful' or even just a sad smile to let you know that they know, I cry. Not full-blown head in the hands wailing, but tears, unstoppable tears.

'Hi Ian, would you like a coffee?'

I could only nod as the now familiar emotion choked me as she guides us back to the sitting area. This phenomenon of strangers contacting you and wanting to help you is uncomfortable, but also inspiring. Other people, like Julie and Jane and now Liz, who have followed the same path, want to reach out to you with words, to acknowledge your circumstances, or to just hold your hand.

'I'm sorry, Liz. Susan didn't feel up to it in the end.'

She poured the coffee. 'Perhaps next time.'

Her husband David arrived and we spent the next three hours talking about grief, Helen and Dominic.

Some people do extraordinary things through grief. Instead of speaking out and condemning the jihadists, Liz and David have spent the last eight years talking to members of the Muslim faith, trying to understand why a young man commits suicide in a public place and ends the lives of twenty-six other people he didn't know. Liz and David are both Christians, and they have approached these discussions with imams and young Muslims alike in a well-balanced and helpful way. Talking to me today, they still couldn't hold back their tears for Helen.

Extraordinary things. On 4 October 2013, two friends dropped their lives and drove from Cheshire to Vicargate. They wanted to be with us, to be close if they were needed. They lived in their camper van on our paddock. They were there on and off for over two months. Inspiring things. Every day for six months, two other friends from Caldbeck brought a cooked meal for us all.

Liz contacted me to share their thoughts on a book of memories for Dominic; they had done something similar for Helen. David also wrote a book of poetry too and I've included one of the poems (Appendix 5) that I strongly identify with.

\*\*\*

The poem, 'My Friend', (Appendix 6) was left at Dom's place anonymously. I tracked the author down. They had laminated the paper and tied it to a small tree, which I thought they had planted. Planting trees is not allowed at the church. I found the poet because I wanted their permission to dig the tree up and replant it somewhere else. As it happens, it was just a broken branch and they had placed in the ground as an anchor so the poem didn't blow away. I'm pretty sure the writer had never written anything like this before. They felt the need to express themselves and write something that would help them. They felt they needed to share their inner thoughts in an attempt to move on.

The poet was very close to Dominic in the months before his death. I imagine that CS Lewis wrote *A Grief Observed* anonymously, for similar reasons to this poet. Their relationship wasn't in the public domain; therefore, names are not required.

\*\*\*

# The Letter to Susan

My Dearest Susan,

After we lost Dominic, I thought I had lost everything; nothing seemed important to me anymore. I thought my world had ended, and as you know I wanted it to. I have watched you from a distance over the last year, and realised that YOU are my everything. You are the heart and the soul of our family and YOU have kept it all together whilst it should have been me.

You are the single most important thing in my life, and I have loved you for thirty-five years.

We have two other talented children and I understand that, but my feelings for what Dom has lost, and what we have lost for not having him here with us has blunted all my other senses. Dom's sudden loss of his life and of his future has haunted me and is the source of my lack of feeling for anything. I miss my eldest son; the ache is unbearable, but what he has lost has consumed me and is by far the worst sadness of all the troubles that we have endured. For every minute of the day, his smiling face is all I have in my head, and many times in the day I want to scream out loud in pain. Sometimes when I'm on my own, I do.

I know we have to search for another life, and I know the only way I can do that is with your strength and your love for me and our family. I need to thank you for being there and for being my wife, my friend and my crutch over the last twelve months. I wouldn't have survived on my own without you, and I know I wouldn't be here today.

With all my love and deepest thanks.

Ian

# A Displacement Activity

Yesterday, I went to Penrith Library for the book launch of Cumbrian writer and neighbour Irvine Hunt. Dom had done some electrical work at his house and he and his wife thought a great deal of him. Like many of our neighbours, Irvine will have seen and heard Dom buzzing around on his quad bike from the age of eleven. As a writer, I'm sure he wouldn't have been too impressed as Dominic's 125cc engine, sounding like a huge chainsaw, broke into his solitude at very strange times of the day and night. However, he spoke well of him as a polite and skilful young man.

Irvine's new book is called *The Ghost Show* and is based on the Biddall family who toured the North of England and the Lake District in the early 1900s with their mysterious and scary ghost show. Despite many in the theatre audience not believing in ghosts, the travelling fairground attraction left them with an element of doubt. After 4 October 2013, I looked everywhere for ghosts, desperately seeking answers and hope about the afterlife. I was looking for the meaning of life, death, God, the Devil, a sign, a forgotten or lost hieroglyphic to guide me so that Dominic and I will meet up again somehow, somewhere. In the spring, I even considered consulting a psychic. Some people find God at this point; some people lose him. I am by faith a Christian currently without a God, and Lindsay, AKA Abdullah Shaheed Jamal, had just found his. Islam and Christianity both believe suicide is an ecclesiastical crime, so what brings us together in a world that doesn't agree with suicide? I can only see that sacrifice is the ultimate price we can pay and that grief is the price we pay for love.

Irvine's book is an enjoyable distraction. I don't believe in ghosts, but I still look for signs: a crab apple falling from a tree and hitting me on the shoulder as I walk down the lane to the church yard. Is that Dom trying to speak to me? Deep down I know I will never see him again, but like Julie I can't help continuing to look. Nor do I believe in a God who takes a loved son, a grandson and a brother. However, I do admire people of faith who believe in a better life, or another life beyond this one. That is the hope, the gamble and the happy ending. They have come to an agreement with their God.

Without Dom in my life there is no point in going on; suicide is the only solution. Lindsay clearly loved his God and he was willing to sacrifice his life to meet him, to be accepted into his house forever. I would, however, question any God that asks one of his flock to take their own life and the lives of other people whilst on a journey to enlightenment. If there is a house of God, a heaven, no-one on this earth deserves to enter it more than Dominic. He lived his life like everything he did was in preparation for it, all the good deeds and kindness, the love, the generosity, the Dom rules. For everyone like me, like Lindsay, love for someone or something, combined with their loss, is a powerful thing and until you embark on it, you don't know what you will do or what you are capable of.

# A Faustian Deal

This time last year, the day before Dom was killed, I had started a two-year master's degree, so at some point I had to produce some course work. There was, however, another story burning in my head after 3 October 2013 that I needed to write. The introduction to this book is that story and it is called Narrow Field of Vision.

After that, going into March 2014, I fully concentrated on my MA, and produced a novel called *One Hundredth*. It's a fictional story of a young sixteen-year-old black kid who lives on a housing estate in the North West. Against all odds he rises to the top of men's international downhill skiing, finally competing in the Winter Olympics – a Billy Elliot meets Cool Runnings kind of plot. It became the focus for my portfolio, the submission for the MA's final semester in May 2015.

I've been lucky. I enjoy writing, which is why I started the course. I wrote my first poem when I was eleven, then wrote consistently until I was twenty-one. There was a sporadic gap then until 2007 when I started a BA (Hons) degree which included a three-year element of creative writing. I churned out a few short stories, but more significantly I had the idea for *One Hundredth*. The idea turned into a screenplay and had sat there since 2009. I re-wrote it as a novel and it was short-listed by Cinnamon Press on 4 October 2014. I have a caring wife of twenty-seven years. I have two intelligent and well-balanced children. But it's the writing, and Dominic's wrath, that has mostly kept me alive. My family is the most important thing in my life, but this has only really been revealed after Dominic's death. Prior to that, we all had very busy lives and to a large extent we took each other for granted.

I don't know what is normal and what isn't now. In my head I'm having an insane conversation with the devil – not with God? I've lost count of the times I've tried to agree a deal with the devil. I thought he would have me in an instant, but the deal on the table wasn't good enough for him. He's got bigger fish to fry. I am willing to trade my life for Dominic's. If the Devil can wind the clock back, put me in the back of the car that night, not Dom, I'd shake his hand. Is that suicide? I'd even accept one more hour with Dominic and then the Devil could do what he wanted with me. But I know the Devil can't deliver; he can't bring Dominic back, even for that one hour. He can't give me one more second with my son that is outside of my head; no-one can. I've known that from day one but in the insanity that is grief, it's normal to seek answers. It's normal to know deep down that I will never see him again. I've even prayed to a God I don't believe in. How can I trust words that were written 2,000 years ago? How can I trust a being that no-one has ever seen; how can I now even believe in Jesus Christ after the last twelve months?

# 5 November 2014

I have tormentors. Persecutors I have to live with for the rest of my life. Julie tells us she still looks for her dad in crowds, fourteen years after his death. I know what she means. Constant reminders of Dominic are everywhere and appear from everything I see, smell or hear. I look for connections to him even if it has no link to him, I make it fit somehow and relate it back to him.

I looked out of the window this morning. It was the first frost. My immediate thought was for Dominic. He would be freezing lying in the ground at St Kentigern's church. It's irrational, but these are the thoughts that crowd out the rational. I don't know how long I stood in the shower; the water was so hot it burned my back. I needed to be punished. Later, I stood at his grave. The tears ran down my cheeks. 'Why punished?' you ask. The answer is 'I wasn't there to protect my son when he needed me.' It's irrational; he wasn't a child that I'd lost sight of on the beach or had wandered onto the balcony of my high rise flat or holiday apartment or, like the stoat, had tried to cross a busy road without my help. He was twenty-two years old. A man who ran his own business and home. He made his own decisions. Why should I constantly beat myself up? Why do I wish every day it was me in the car, not him? Why wasn't I there to protect him?

When Dom went off to Lanzarote to work at seventeen, we went out within a week or two to make sure everything was okay. He came to find our hotel on the first day. He sat next to me on a lounger by the pool, and it was good to see him. He didn't take his shirt off to sunbathe. He told us later that day that he had impetigo, and my heart ached for him. There was no way he would have come home and I wouldn't have asked him to. This image now blurs as I try to recall our conversations throughout the rest of that day on the Island. I wish now I had insisted he come home. We would have had another six months with him.

Alcohol, the deadliest tormentor, the disintegration of my relationship with my wife, constant flashbacks of Dominic or my mum, life without either, living life with myself. Any white van, small children, hoodies, any music –

although some songs strike deeper than others. These are all tormentors and there are many. Demons that we face in our quest to leave the shadow that our loved one's death casts across our lives. Are we blighted? Are we destined to suffer these ghosts forever?

\*\*\*

I had my last bereavement session with Colin on 21 October 2014. I hadn't seen him all summer; we agreed to have a break. As I was leaving and saying a final goodbye, he recommended I read a book written by Julian Barnes called *Levels of Life*. Julian's wife and literary agent, Pat Kavanagh, died on 20 October 2008. The book published in 2013 is divided into three parts: part history, part wistful essay and fictionalised biography, and the third part is a grief memoir about the death of his wife. The pieces combine to form a fascinating narrative about love, grief and other things that have never been joined or connected together before. Many of the emotions and descriptions of his feelings in the book mirror what Julie and Jane have described to me about the loss of their dad. Barnes writes about his isolation for a while, and the moment he realised why he wouldn't kill himself:

> Or rather, the sudden arriving argument – which made it less likely that I would kill myself. I realised that insofar as she was alive at all, she was alive in my memory. Of course, she remains powerfully in other people's minds as well; but I was her principal rememberer. If she was anywhere, she was within me, internalised. This was normal. And it was equally normal – and irrefutable – that I could not kill myself because then I would also be killing her. (p. 90)

We need to find reasons to stay alive, to keep our loved one's memory alive, and as Barnes writes, that is his reason. But every day, many times a day, when you remember that they are dead and you'll never see them again, the anxiety attack strikes – the moment it hits you, there's a sharp intake of breath, the gasp, a pain somewhere in your being, and then, when you can breathe again there is the familiar thought: 'I can't go on; I can't live with this pain anymore.' The wave passes, and Dom's smiling face returns once more to haunt you. Your life becomes invisible again, and you return to living in the shadow.

***

I am a writer, and my instincts are to create believable characters and write an exciting narrative arc. In this story the characters are based on real events. Names haven't been changed to protect the innocent and I haven't created fictional characters to create dramatic effect. Dominic is my protagonist, his death and my survival are the arc, and I'm living, creating and recording it, even now as I write in a Liverpool university.

AS Byatt, in *Possession: A Romance* (1990), wrote, 'the individual appears for an instant, joins the community of thought, modifies it, and dies; but the species, that dies not, reaps the fruit of his ephemeral existence.' I feel like that. I learned so much from Dominic over the short period we worked together, I could agree and argue that 'I'm a writer; that's what writers do', but is writing about his death and how I deal with it a self-help book, or is it art for art's sake? I don't necessarily want to open up this nineteenth century 'l'art pour l'art' wound, but I need to. It cuts across the fundamental argument of why we endeavour artistically to create a work that helps in the grieving process.

James McNeill Whistler (1834-1903), artist and a leading proponent of the credo 'art for art's sake', wrote the following in which he discarded the accustomed role of art in the service of the state or official (Catholic) religion: (Even prior to the 'life verses art' philosophical topos raging between the bohemians, the debate went further back to the sixteenth century and the Catholic Reformation)

> Art should be independent of all claptrap – should stand alone [...] and appeal to the artistic sense of eye or ear, without confounding this with emotions entirely foreign to it, as devotion, pity, love, patriotism and the like. (*Art for art's sake*, Victor Cousin (1792–1867) – l'Art pour l'art)

Whistler was challenging the teachings of John Ruskin and the later advocates of Social Realism who thought that the value of art was to serve a moral or didactic purpose. This view is also taken by Edgar Allan Poe in one of his last essays, *The Poetic Principle* (1850):

> We have taken it into our heads that to write a poem simply for the poem's sake [...] and to acknowledge such to have been our design, would be to confess ourselves radically wanting in the true poetic dignity and force: – but the simple fact is that would we but permit ourselves to look into our own souls we should immediately there discover that under the sun there neither exists nor can exist any work more thoroughly dignified, more supremely noble, than this very poem, this poem per se, this poem which is a poem and nothing more, this poem written solely for the poem's sake. (para. 12)

On the other hand, in his book *Twilight of the Idols* (1889) Friedrich Nietzsche suggests that 'Art is the great stimulus to life: how could one understand it as purposeless, as aimless, as l'art pour l'art?' (p. 71) Nietzsche argues that the fight against purpose in art is always a fight against the moralising tendency in art, against its subservience to morality. He writes, 'L'art pour l'art means, 'The devil take morality!'' (p. 71), but suggests that one question remains: 'art also makes apparent much that is ugly, hard, and questionable in life; does it not thereby spoil life for us?

As a parent I make no moral, religious or political arguments for my grief. I see the unnecessary death of Dominic as being as ugly as it gets. As a writer, however, I see it as an opportunity to write passionately about something I'm experiencing but don't understand. It's certainly not to make a political statement or moralise, and it's certainly not, as Poe suggests, written for its own sake. But I realise I need to establish who the creator of the work is and who is its hero? Is it what Dominic did and achieved in his life? Is it me, chronicling it? Or is it a father and son collaboration?

# To smile, or not to smile?

In the beginning I resigned myself to dying twice, to never being happy or smiling again. But over the last year in my search for a response to Dom's death, reading Nietzsche, Poe, Whistler, Orwell and others, have provided solace. I've written thousands of words including the literary corpses that inhabit my pending work in progress and now, as an academic, I smile with acquiescence. As a writer, though, I would rather argue that I'm a grieving parent, and want to use what skills I have in that role, to remember my son in a loving and lasting way. However self-absorbed I've been over the last few years – I read here 'how sorry I've felt for myself' – I am also an autoethnographer researching creativity, grief and depression. I want to say through my writing to others along the way, who may also have lost a loved one, 'Please, write: write anything; write everything; it doesn't matter. It helped me when I was you.'

At the start, I tried to write everything down that I could remember about Dominic, especially about the pain.

The images that shot across my eyes were normally of an innocent boy. Sometimes just smiling at the camera, playing in the snow or banging nails into a piece of wood. What words can express or describe the death of your child?

Thankfully this experience is completely alien to most people. The more I wrote, the more I discussed the work openly and the more grieving people wrote or talked to me. I realised that it was important to identify with people like these and we perhaps could gain some comfort in discussing our loss.

I felt that at the same time as making a scholarly contribution with my Ph.D. research, it was also important for me to share any insights and perhaps Dom's story with them, particularly if they felt isolated as I did and were limited in the ways they could communicate or explain their loss. Everyone reads, right?

The initial impulses to write came to me in waves; they were multi-sensory and multi-voiced. A word, an image, an object, even the weather, caused me to write. I needed to write something, anything, so I didn't forget my son. Often, the writing was painful but I wanted and needed to feel the pain. I mustn't forget my son. Grief does this, especially in relation to an early and unexpected death.

At the beginning, it didn't matter if the words went into the memoir, on a scrap of paper or into the Ph.D. critical analysis; it was just one monologue of sadness.

# Dom's baby?

'What's this?' I point to a letter on the kitchen table.

'It's an appointment on Monday, an eye specialist. The vet thinks that Lucy has a tumour on one eye and ulcers on the other one,' Susan says. Lucy, Dom's border collie, is a living link to his life outside our memories of him. Not a photo or video, a breathing single thread connection to his adult life. Lucy, the companion that travelled with him in his car daily, and walked at his side.

I have a fantasy, and sometimes it feels too real. Dominic wasn't fond of children. I often had to remind him that he was one once. He would look at me sideways, and smile. It was more to do with the business. He never liked them running around the bar, dropping chips and veg all over the floor and running sticky, jammy fingers all over the windows and curtains. I could see where he was coming from on that one, but that was down to parenting, and a far cry from the way Dominic and his siblings were brought up. Nonetheless, he had, and showed, respect for everyone and everything, regardless of their upbringing, sex, creed or colour, another of Dom's rules. He reminds me of that joke:

> There's a man walking down a corridor and he opens the door for a woman.
>
> 'You don't need to do that just because I'm a lady,' she says haughtily.
>
> 'I'm not,' he replies, 'I'm doing it because I'm a gentleman.'

He always did the right thing instinctively and calmly. I still can't look at pictures of him where he's always smiling. I can't comprehend how Susan and I made such a beautiful person, inside and out, and he's gone, taken from us, and all we have left are the pictures and his dog, Lucy. I have this one fantasy. One sunny afternoon I'm sitting here at my desk as I am now, looking out into the orchard and across the fields. The roses are in bloom and I can see the damsons on the trees. A car pulls up, a silver one, but I can't see the make.

The driver sits in the car, head bowed. It's a woman. I sip my coffee and the driver's door opens, the sunlight bounces off the window and dazzles me. She opens the rear passenger door and leans in. She backs out with a bundle in her arms, closes both doors. I can see clearly again. She can't see me watching from the study, but she walks towards the porch door, nervous. She stands for a few seconds and then knocks.

I open the front door. She's pretty; she smiles. There's a baby in her arms. She speaks.

'You don't know me. I was a friend of Dom's.'

I run this scenario in my head all the time. She doesn't always knock on the front door. Sometimes she stops me in the deli section in the supermarket; she has a baby in a sling across her breasts. Or I'm walking towards her in the park; she's pushing a pram and I can see she is hesitant. It's a fantasy, but, at the moment at least, we still have Lucy.

\*\*\*

The eye specialist says that Lucy has an immune system problem; it's attacking her cornea and causing blood vessels to grow across them. We have been given drops that are designed for humans but have been successful in reversing the growth in dogs. Lucy hates them and we can't get near her to take them. I have resorted to dropping them on my thumb and massaging them into her lower eye lid. The vet has advised us not to do this as it's a steroid; it's dangerous and gloves should be worn. What do I do? We can't afford for Lucy to lose her eyesight. We can't lose our living thread to Dom.

\*\*\*

Dominic's headstone is the first one you see as you walk past the car park of St Kentigern's church. Or it just might be the first one I look for. Either way, I get a longing to the point of pain in my chest whenever it comes into view. Today, as usual, the church is deserted. Even though St Kentigern's is in the next field but one to Vicargate, it's still a twenty-minute walk around to it, but not a single car passed me. I lift the latch and place it back down silently as I close the gate. The sun is shining but the grass is wet. I let the dogs off their leads as I draw level with Marion Davidson's resting place, a neighbour from Sowerby Hall. I see the back of a new memento placed in front of Dominic's stone; it immediately stands out amongst the flowers and other keepsakes. It's a hardboard sign about twelve inches square, anchored to the ground with those small canes that keep tomato plants straight.

It happens all the time: things are left, flowers, poems and keepsakes, often anonymously. The church is off the beaten track but people always find their way here. Some folk like to chat with him like me, or just pay their respects. As I draw level with the new gift, I prepare to read a heartfelt message. Within the hour I'm at the police station with the 'message' in a plastic bag. The police officer is shocked that someone could even contemplate going to a church with hate in the heart to violate a holy place.

*** 

# A letter arrives on 7 May 2015

National Offender Management Services
6 May 2015
ENSURING THE VICTIM MATTERS
VICTIM LIAISON UNIT

Dear Mr Loftus,

There have been some developments in the case in which you were involved. Given this, would you please ring me either on the number above or on my direct line 0300 XXXXXX

Yours sincerely

Sarah
Victim Liaison Officer

I ring the number, leave a message and the liaison officer calls me back the next day.

'Morning, Mr Loftus, Sarah here. I hope you're well. This is just a request and part of the rehabilitation process; you don't have to say yes.'

Sarah first rang me in March, informing me that my son's killer would be released in about two years, only serving half of the sentence. 'Do you want to set up any restrictions?' she said, almost as a consolation prize. My first instinct this time was that she was going to tell me the release date was even sooner.

'We have received a request that Glendinning wants to see, or write to you and say sorry.' She said it almost apologetically, half sensing what my response would be.

As calmly as I could, I said 'No.' It wasn't our wish to meet our son's killer. I explained what had happened the day before at Dominic's grave. Whilst it wasn't the killer who placed the message, it was clearly someone within his circle. Someone was holding a grudge for whatever bizarre, twisted reason. The victim liaison officer was also shocked at this indecent act, and she didn't pursue the request further. I told her the police were involved and had possession of the sign, but I had taken a photo on my phone. She asked for a copy. I sent it to her the next day, accompanied by a letter outlining our reasons for saying 'No' to the request.

\*\*\*

Vicargate,
9 May 2015.

Dear Sarah,

RE: GLENDINNING'S REQUEST TO APOLOGISE TO THE LOFTUS FAMILY BY LETTER OR IN PERSON

I refer to our conversation yesterday informing us of the above request. As we discussed, I confirm my initial response of 'No' to this contact and shall justify why in this letter.

Susan and I discussed this after you rang, and in our opinion, this is an empty gesture. Up to this point he has shown no remorse to the police, to us, to the other two men in the car, who were seriously injured, or their parents. In fact, it was quite the opposite; leading up to the trial he, his brother and friends harassed my daughter and her friends, which is on police record, and also blamed Dominic for his own demise.

We appreciate this request is part of the rehabilitation process, but our feeling is that Glendinning just offering to apologise has already 'ticked the box'.

This is not a vindictive decision; we are very much a humanitarian family and after Dominic was killed, we set up a charity called the 'Cumbrian Lad'. This is relevant when you look at the photograph enclosed with this letter we discussed on the call. The charity was initially set up to help students leaving school.

The following are reasons why we will not be taking this request forward:

Glendinning denied everything and pleaded 'not guilty' with the defence of 'I can't remember anything after getting behind the steering wheel.'

He waited until the morning of the trial to plea bargain due to overwhelming evidence, with a guilty plea to a lesser charge. How can he say sorry for something he says he can't remember?

We have had promises from Glendinning before. Dominic caught him sniffing cocaine in our bar and ejected him under threat of calling the Police. He came back six weeks later and apologised to me and told me he was now 'clean'. I accepted his apology, but we know from that friendship group that the drugs didn't stop and prior to imprisonment he was seen going in and out of a well-known drug dealer's house in Penrith.

The desecration of Dominic's grave over the Bank Holiday weekend. I have transcribed the wording on the enclosed photograph, which reads as follows:

> 'Lad was not always good Dad
> If he had done his job right on the night
> He wood (sic) not be where he is tonight'
> E L

We clearly can't prove or blame anyone specifically and have reported this to the Police, who are going to try to recover forensics. XXXX had made those two points on Facebook and in telephone texts to my daughter. It appears to be too much of a coincidence, in our view.

Finally, Glendinning was given a seven-year prison sentence reduced to five because of the guilty plea, despite it being on the morning of the trial. Then, this is reduced to two years six months to give more time for his 'rehabilitation'.

We do not want to be involved in a process that circumnavigates the justice system even further. By offering the victim's family an empty gesture to get a further reduction, in our view, is immoral. It is offensive to us and we will never forgive the killer of our son.

Perhaps certain people can be rehabilitated, but equally some people are just bad and go on to continually offend; the statistics are there to prove that. In fact, the answer to this problem is in the statistics:

58% of prisoners serving 1 year or less re-offend
36% re-offend serving 2-4 years
26% re-offend serving 4-10 years
16% re-offend serving over 10 years

Whilst we know it's not practical, due to lack of space and prisons, it is clear longer sentences reduce crime. However, as part of this restorative justice system any contact by the offender with the victims has to be dangerous, and may not help the offender or the victim.

Yours sincerely

Ian Loftus

# 2 June 2015 'Courage is a peculiar kind of fear'

Today for the second time in a few days I've used the phrase 'There by the grace of God…' The demon, the elephant in the room, blinked, an eyebrow raised. My black beast takes a throat-clearing cough, then confidently announces its presence like a peacock assured of its sexuality, spreads its wings and splashes itself all over Sky News, Twitter, and Facebook and will no doubt be in every UK newspaper tomorrow.

Charles Kennedy, the ex-Liberal Democrat leader, died today at the age of fifty-five. His demon, his bête noire, and now his executioner, alcohol. I have long been an admirer of Kennedy, but I've seen the look and effects of heavy drinking in his face. The tired look, the look that replaced the fresh-faced MP of the early 1990s, puffy blepharitic eyes and cheeks of excess and late sessions. The look of superior intellect confused, influenced but contaminated by another higher-in-ABV contributor.

Writers, intellectuals and academics have argued that they have expanded their thinking by its presence; it might be so, but by God Charles could run rings around his political contemporaries, with or without it. Live hard and die young? But be remembered for your spirited repartee, banter and deep philosophical Claret-formed opinion? (God, it reads less convincingly when you read it back the next day, sober.) That's the third time I've used the word 'God'. It's a Habit. I will come back to God later.

Habit, like arriving home after work, late, having taken six hours to drive from London to Penrith, needing the toilet but needing to get home more. Even before the cistern has finished flushing, the cork is pulled and the southern levels of stress are subsiding.

'It's a school night,' she says.

'Yeah, but I've been in my car since five o'clock and my head's still buzzing.' A pattern-forming habit.

But it was different for Charles, and it's different for people who do not have control, lost or otherwise.

There is a dichotomy with drinking. I like and enjoy a fine wine; I appreciate its balanced flavours with a meal. I have enjoyed a cognac and a good cigar. I have felt the uplift of a Jägermeister at the end of a long, steep red ski run in Saalbach. But I've also been on my hands and knees in the pantry, consumed with desperation at two or three o'clock in the morning, looking in the cupboard for anything vaguely alcoholic to feed the demon. Then, woken up on the sofa in the half light, the half-full glass of cooking sherry still in my hand. The demon has shit in my mouth and I despise it, and myself.

What is the hunger and where does it come from? Why is there a craving to have another drink? Is it liquid armour against the pain, the loss, the regret, the guilt and the anger? Do you have these emotions even though you haven't lost anyone and you're not grieving? It's too late to ask Charles Kennedy, so I sit here alone. It's 1.05 am and everyone is in bed. I've been drinking every day for weeks without a break, but never during the day. Is that the next step in the race to the bottom? Charles tried many times to control the demon, and failed. His son came along in 2005 and he was even more determined to give up his addiction, but failed again, permanently.

So, to God? It's hard to remember, but I had a life before 3 October 2013. A good life, and in this madness, after the failed deal with the devil, I have spoken with 'God' to try to help understand where it's all gone wrong. I had a perfect life: three beautiful children, a beautiful home, a healthy relationship – we've loved each other since we were kids – and decent, hardworking friends. Many of these things still remain in place, but without Dominic, none of it remains in place, including God; that's if he ever had a place.

# Rose Cottage, Gower

I started listening to music again when Susan and I drove down to South Wales in the summer of 2015. It was a long journey from the Lakes and for the first time in nearly two years, I tentatively turned the volume up on the car radio. Barry White – *You're the First, the Last, my Everything* (1974) – was playing. I've always appreciated all types of music, from Mozart to Marley and everything in between. It was a simple pleasure, yet that day it felt like a very guilty pleasure. Sade's *Love Deluxe* (1992), one of my all-time favourite albums, played next. Dom was one year old when it was released. I played the CD often in the car as he grew up. As I listened to the music, I had that 'dinner plate in the sink' moment when the Police were leaving Vicargate. How can I enjoy such things when I always find within them a tenuous link back to Dom? Even the old disco classic with Barry White takes me back to when I was Dom's age and it makes me think of him. I switched the radio off.

# Anniversaries

We were approached by Cumbria Police at the start of December 2015. They asked if we wanted to help in their Christmas Drink Drive TV campaign. With real sadness but purpose we arrived at the Police media department and we were sat down in front of a camera. We had a few days to prepare. The Police had already emailed us a couple of specific questions that they wanted to cover in the interview.

After we sat down, it was literally: 'Are you ready? One, two, three, go.' And the camera started rolling. The young policeman didn't want to drag it out any longer than necessary. As best we could, we explained to the camera that we were supporting the campaign because as a family, we were at the extreme end of the devastation caused by a drink driving incident. It was a week night in October and Dom had been working in the kitchen. Susan was with him just before he started his shift. He read out a Trip Advisor comment about our restaurant and they laughed together. That was the last time she saw him alive. I'd seen him that morning when we'd taken his car to the garage. After his shift, Dom got into a car driven by a twenty-three-year-old man who thought he was beyond the law after drinking five pints and two whiskies. Two years later, emotionally, we were no further forward. We were still in pain. It nearly destroyed us as a couple. We had struggled to deal with each other's grief; we were very different types of people and we each found it hard to cope with how the other was handling Dominic's death. Friends and customers who saw us still living our lives might have thought we were over it. They had no idea. My mind and body functioned on a day-to-day basis but I didn't feel my heart beat any more. Our lives were now just an existence.

We only got up in the morning because we had Chloe and Reuben to think about. They were suffering too, but I felt they couldn't express their grief because they knew it would upset us. Even now Chloe imagines that Dominic is at another place, at work, or with his friends. She was fortunate enough to have built an adult relationship with her elder brother; Reuben wasn't that lucky. He felt Dom was just getting to know him as his friend rather than his annoying little brother. Nowadays, he loses himself in his music and is fortunate to have that creative outlet. The songs he writes often show his inner feelings. Both Chloe and Reuben have been incredibly strong and whilst they are not over Dom's death they are trying to get on with their lives.

The police asked us about the effect of Dom's death on friends as well as family. We replied that friends and family had been totally supportive. They have been there for us every day of the last two years. Dom had a lot of friends too, who still mourn and remember him with great respect and affection. They lost their 'main man', as they called him. They won't ever forget him but they will hopefully live their lives to the full knowing that would have been what Dominic wanted.

The policeman also asked if we had a message for people over Christmas? Susan gave the obvious response: 'Don't drink and drive. When you're out having a good time, you might think it's only a couple of festive drinks. What's the worst that can happen? It's not about losing your licence, your job or being fined; that's bad enough. It's about what effect causing an accident may have on someone's family as well as your own. You have to live with what you have done, as does the victim's family.

This campaign is usually promoted at Christmas and New Year but it's a message for 365 days of the year. Christmas is a time to celebrate. Do not let it turn into a time to mourn.' Susan leant into the camera, 'No parent should have to plan their child's funeral at any time but especially not after a tragic and needless accident. Prevent this heartache from happening to another family. Be responsible. Please don't drink and drive. If you're suspicious and think that someone has been drinking, report it to the Police. Potentially, reporting someone for drink driving could save someone else's life, and that could be a member of your family or close friend.'

Susan looked away from the camera. 'I would give anything to hear Dominic say 'Mam' once more.'

Finally, she said, 'At this time of year we think about the nativity, Christmas gifts and twinkling lights. They are symbols that remind us that Christmas is really about the birth of Christ. Please, don't let Christmas be the symbol for the rest of your life that you killed or seriously injured someone.'

# Minus One

Last night was the night before Christmas Eve. The night of the Sportsmans traditional Christmas party with live music until midnight. The Loftus family have hosted the party for five years now, with the same musical duo performing a lively compilation of Christmas songs, classic covers and the odd Irish drinking song. It was always a room full of fun, seasonal happiness, family, friends old and new, and bubbly festive cheer. Last night's celebration was another night without Dominic. Another night of guilt.

As a parent, I have always blamed myself for Dominic's death. I think every parent who loses a child does so at some point. This is slightly at odds with Kübler-Ross and her five stages of grief. One of the stages she discusses is an 'anger' phase, and 'blame' as an emotion falls within it. In this case she means we blame someone else. And of course, I do, the drunk driver who killed Dominic. But should I blame Dom too, for getting in the car? He knew better.

I mentioned earlier that Dr Elizabeth Kübler Ross's book *On Death and Dying* (1969) is not about grief but about patients who are terminally ill or coming to the end of their lives. I reference it, because it can be argued that the five stages a dying person can experience: denial, anger, bargaining, depression and finally acceptance, are also emotions that someone grieving can experience. Although, more latterly, Strobe and Shut (1999) suggested that the five stages of Kübler Ross's grieving process are too orderly to reflect just how messy grief can be. We can grieve in other circumstances, not just after the death of a loved one. We can experience grief when moving house, being made redundant or after a divorce. I wondered if the drunk driver had grieved. The twelve months before he went to trial, he was certainly in denial. He was also drinking and driving two nights before he killed Dominic. He offered Dom a lift home after a pool game at the Oddfellows, and Dom refused. Dom said to another friend after the driver had left, 'He's a knob, and he's going to kill someone one day.' The guilt breaks my heart, knowing that the someone was Dominic.

Of course, I don't blame Dom, but I've had even stranger thoughts since his death. My life revolves around my grief; I need the pain to remind myself that he's not here anymore. That pain is fuelled by questions that will never be answered, by 'what ifs'. What if I hadn't encouraged him to be part of my dream? What if I had worked that night and not him? What if he hadn't got in the car? What if I hadn't bought this bar and restaurant against Susan's advice? What if…?

There are many other 'what ifs'; they run through my thoughts every day, and last night was no exception. This time it was framed as 'if only'. 'If only he was here.' Yesterday evening, over two years later, when all his friends are full of life, dancing, drinking, getting engaged and partying, his mother still weeps silently in the corner. I still can only blame myself.

## July 2016 – Vicargate

There's a photo of Dom and Linzi on the piano at the bottom of the stairs. On the way to bed, I normally look away from it as I walk past. Tonight, for some reason I stopped. The photo is in a blue ceramic frame. Dom is wearing a dark suit and tie; Linzi is wearing a blue cocktail dress. It's almost the same colour as the frame. It was taken on his eighteenth birthday and they're both smiling at the photographer. Did I take it? I can't remember. On the other side of the room, there's only a table lamp illuminating, so the photo is in half shadow. Dom didn't own a tie so I lean in for a closer look. I smile back at him, wryly. It's one of mine.

I'm typing in bed, thinking about Dominic. Trying to remember what else he was doing when he was eighteen. He had not long returned from Lanzarote and was getting ready to start his electrician's apprenticeship at college. It reminded me that I didn't go to college and I tried to remember what I was doing at that age. As I recall, I too was at a crossroads. That quickly takes me back to my father's house in Euston Street, Liverpool, forty years earlier almost to the day.

When you're eighteen, you can't contemplate forty years in the future; you hardly think forty hours ahead. You live in the moment. At some point you'll look back at your life, like David, the old man who stands on the other side of the Sportsmans bar on a Saturday night, staring into his glass. At a lull during service, he looks up and says, 'You kids have never had it so good. When I was your age, we didn't even have electricity, and after the war, we had no food either. But life was good and I'm still alive.'

This conversation over the bar is one reason that I need to feel the pain. I torture myself by thinking about my long life, remembering some of the wonderful experiences I've had, including three beautiful children. I've visited places in every corner of the planet, I've met fascinating people, tasted all kinds of food and wine. I've enjoyed fifty-eight years jam packed with sensations, new things, old things, love, life and laughter. So, like music, how can I appreciate these things anymore when I know Dominic didn't experience many of them in his life?

***

I'm struck by the clarity of the image as I remember my dad's house. A small mid-terrace: the front door opens into a narrow corridor which leads to an even narrower kitchen. The smell of Christa, his wife from Hamburg, and the Teutonic trinkets and sounds of Hamburg that she brought with her almost forty years before that: Die Fledermaus, sauerkraut and apple strudel. Dominic wouldn't be born for another twenty years but I place him there. I invite him to enjoy my happy memories, to get to know his granddad, and perhaps try to make up for the memories that he now won't have, by sharing mine? He wouldn't enjoy sauerkraut and Die Fledermaus, but he would have loved the apple pie. Is this what we do in our grief after the death of our children?

Superimpose our loved one into other aspects of our lives where they have no place to be or couldn't possibly be? Give them our memories because they didn't live long enough to generate those memories themselves?

My thoughts move from the city back to Vicargate. Dom may not have enjoyed classical music, but he did have a happy and idyllic childhood living in the countryside. I wanted him to have a happy adulthood too. Despite the fact that Dominic was killed on a quiet country road, one of the greatest pleasures of bringing children up in the country is the freedom. Not just the freedom and feeling of open space, but the freedom to be able to roam the lanes, fields, forests and fells without coming to any harm. The freedom for them to do naive experiments, the freedom to understand the fundamentals of life as they witness nature and natural things around them, without political spin or correctness. The freedom of just being able to piss over the fence.

# February 2017

Guilt. I felt it in 1997 when Dom was six. I wrote a poem between Christmas and New Year just after Reuben was born and just before Dom's birthday. Reuben was a Christmas baby born at a happy time, but it made me realise that Dom was nearly seven and I hardly knew him. The guilt then was a different kind of guilt from the guilt I feel now. It was an absent father's guilt felt by many young dads, of working too hard and not spending enough time with their children. In our case, Monday to Friday away from home, and Saturday morning at 6 am, a little boy bouncing up and down on your bed wanting to play with his dad. You're totally knackered, with a list of jobs as long as your arm to do in the money pit. Then the journey back to London on Sunday night or early Monday morning.

In her book, Kübler-Ross hardly touches on guilt, but as an emotion it's the one that has dominated the last three years of my life. Perhaps it's re-awakened my feeling from when Dom was a boy of seven, and amplified it? Although it's only three years, three months and one day since he was killed, I know that for me, guilt is a thread that dominates my grief, and will be with me for the rest of my life. Every time I go to see Dom, I tell him that I would give anything to swap our positions. Wishing it was me in the ground, and he was coming to tell me what he's been doing.

He'd be twenty-six now, and often when I stand with him at his grave, I talk to him, and tell him the latest news, but I also wonder what he would be like today. Not just physically, but what stage would he be at in his life? Would he have his own family? Girls or boys? What would their names be? And I often wonder if he would have got back with his ex- and long-time girlfriend, Linzi?

At the time of the car crash, Linzi was working in Leeds as a paediatric nurse and had moved away a few months earlier. She couldn't get the job she wanted in Cumbria and Leeds was the nearest option. This move was a big influence on their separation. I do know, however, that they had arranged to meet at the Chill Factor ski centre in Manchester on the following Monday after he was killed. Today, I found that poem I'd written about Dom. It was loose in the back of an A4 note pad. After I read it, I hit a wall, a newer, higher, thicker wall, a now insurmountable wall of guilt.

***

The victim liaison officer rang again at 12 o'clock today on 3 March 2017. I was expecting the call at some point this month, but it still came as a blood-stopping, brain-freezing kick in the groin.

She came straight to the point. 'He's getting released today,' and the memories came back, wave after wave. I drowned in the anguish of them all over again. As I sank below the surface, her voice dimmed to white noise. I started to think about revenge for the first time, about taking his life and ending it short as he did to Dominic. But I'm more in control of myself than he was of his car. It will be slow and very painful. I'd be curious to know how his family might react if he too left them suddenly:

'He was a wonderful, thoughtful son,' they would say. 'How could someone do this to him?'

Everyone else knew he was a dirt-bag; he needed killing. But surely, even in their narrow, innocent perspective, unwrinkled in their unconditional love and their parental blindness, they should suffer as I have? It wouldn't be murder, would it? I could plead insanity, diminished responsibility. It would be viewed as an accident if he was crossing the road at the same time that I was driving past, at speed. Or even better, I could do it under the cover of darkness, hiding down a dark alley with a cricket bat. Later, burning the blood-stained willow on the pub's open fire, the evidence destroyed.

As if my thoughts couldn't get any darker, I thought about other options. Like paying someone. On one hand, that's probably more dangerous than doing it myself, because now two people would know my plans. However, a professional would be more clinical, less emotional. They would make fewer mistakes. He or she would be more likely to have the right equipment: a gun with the serial code filed off, a stiletto, my weapon of choice, or an undetectable poison, slipped into his beer at the Station Hotel in Penrith. This toxin doesn't have an antidote, but it kills slowly and painfully. All major organs shut down. He bleeds from his ears, his nose and his arse, Ha! I smile at this method. Yes, he's fucked and his friends can only watch as he dies very slowly.

After recent events at Kuala Lumpur airport, my contractor might contemplate a VX nerve agent. It was very successful, but the finger was automatically pointed at the leader of North Korea. That wouldn't do – I would be on the police's suspect list straightway: I'd have motive and, they would argue, opportunity. So, I would ask the killer to pass on this method. Yes, it's deadly, but in hindsight it would be over too quickly, at least for my liking. Where would he get it, anyway, unless he had contacts at the highest level in Pyongyang? It's rumoured that Kim Yong-un is paranoid. He sees his relatives as a threat to his rule, and it was he who ordered the murder of Kim Yong-nam. He wasn't the first of the Korean leader's relatives to die mysteriously. What's the difference between fratricide, avunculicide or employing a virucide? I'm not paranoid and I don't feel threatened, but at this point I am contemplating organising, planning and hiring someone to do my dirty work. I think about a 'no win no fee' type arrangement, like mis-sold PPI. The terminator would need to provide proof that the contract was complete, such as photos of the dead target in a pool of blood with a copy of the day's Daily Telegraph on his chest. Perhaps a head shot with his testes in his mouth? Even better, his head on a platter, brought back to the pub in the dead of night, cash in hand, no questions.

The social worker's voice rises above the white noise. 'If I can be of any help, you've got my number. He's under the same bail conditions as before.'

How the hell can she help, when I'm drowning?

'Actually, maybe she can,' I think to myself. 'Who's the most violent, unbalanced and disturbed person on her probation list? Who does she know that has no remorse and has killed before?' She could text you his number. Then again, he might not be around very long as I dream the ironic dream and start the plan in my head.

# A Stay of Execution

I'd never heard of the term Survivor Advocacy (SA) until Prof. Carla Sofka contacted me from Siena College, Albany, NY. I'd cited her work, *Social Support Internetworks, Caskets for Sale, and More: Thanatology and the Information Superhighway* (1997) in the bibliography I uploaded to Academia.com supporting my Ph.D. abstract. Carla coined the phrase and has promoted the idea of 'thanatechnology' since 1997. She defines it as 'communication technology used in the provision of death education, grief counselling and Thanatology research.' Essentially, it's any kind of technology that can be used to deal with death, dying, grief, loss and illness. Since then, the internet of things is now virtually running our lives. We have apps for everything and we live and communicate our personal lives via social media. Carla couldn't have envisaged how quickly 'Grief Tech' would evolve, or how established and normal, apps such as Afternote would become.

Survivor Advocacy is not just about grief. It's a therapeutic process to support a survivor or victim of any trauma ranging from the death of a loved one, rape, sexual or violent abuse, to supporting a car crash survivor. A common theme for most trauma victims is the feeling of being powerless. A rape survivor by default is unable to stop the attacker. The patient is encouraged to talk about their experience, which is part of the healing process and aims to try to give them back a sense of power, meaning and independence. For me, if I had the power, I would have stopped Dom getting into the car, but I wasn't there so I couldn't. If I had the power, his killer wouldn't be free today.

I've not spoken with an advocate yet; I don't suppose I ever will, but Carla's email made me re-think my plan about engaging a hitman. She had shown me that rather than cutting off someone's testicles and putting them in their mouth like a Mexican drugs cartel hit, some grieving people do wonderful things because of, or in spite of, their grief. She didn't explain it to me that way, but on the other hand, she didn't know I had a blunt instrument in my pocket, 'just in case the moment presented itself'.

Of course, I'm not a violent man. We all have dark thoughts but rarely do we act on them. Nonetheless, how far could someone be pushed before they do? What happens when your moral compass is so caught up in the magnetic storm that is grief and all direction is lost? What happens when you suffer something so traumatic that everything in your life has no meaning or value?

As I compiled a list of undetectable poisons, I started to think about *Groundhog Day* (1993) again, and Phil, stuck in his timeless loop. Prior to his reporting assignment to Punxsutawney, he too felt no value to his life. He had no direction. At some point, during his repetitive days, he realised that his memories of 2 February were intact, but the town lived it every time for the first time, so his actions had no long-term consequences for him. He started to enjoy this, and made the most of his freedom: seducing beautiful women, stealing money, even drink driving and a police chase. He attempted to seduce Rita and failed. He began to tire of, and then dread, his existence.

In an attempt to break the cycle, he drove a stolen truck into a quarry and killed himself but the loop still didn't stop. He committed suicide several times. He electrocuted himself. He stepped in front of a truck on the road and jumped from a tall building, but his death could not stop the day from repeating. He tried to seduce Rita once again. He asked what she wanted in a man, which was someone who was humble, kind, generous, courageous and sensitive, someone who liked children, someone who loved his mother and played a musical instrument. He pretended to like these things too. When he finally started to be honest, she became more receptive. He explained the loop he was stuck in and convinced her with his extensive knowledge of future events to come. After he opened his heart, her advice helped him to gradually find a goal for his directionless life.

# Moving On?

On 23 October 2017, with regret, we accepted an offer on Vicargate. We needed to start packing the house contents. I lowered the ladder and put the light on in the loft that spans the house. It contained three decades of memories and artifacts that chronologically record the lives of our three children. There was however, no (chronological) rhyme or reason to the packing of the boxes in the loft. There was no organisation. Unlike the house boxes with the names of origin on the top or side – kitchen, dining room or bathroom – the loft boxes were blank. Over the years, as toys were discarded, they were packed away, sometimes in their original packing, never to be played with again. We brought them down into the kitchen to sift through them. Like the contents of the house, we had to decide what was to go the tip or the charity shop and what we would keep. Unpacking the loft to pack for the move was an emotional lottery. With each reveal, the item would spark its own flash of memory. I didn't want to be the one to bring a box down, open it to discover it was Dom's VHS tapes and DVDs. As I brought the boxes down, Susan was packing away the books. There were books in every room in the house, including the kitchen. Eventually, there was a pile of about twenty boxes of books to go into storage and a pile to go to the charity shop. I picked up the first one in the charity pile to put in the back of my car. It was heavy and I put it down again and opened it. I recognised the book on the top straight away by its green dust cover and yellow writing. It was *Wind in the Willows* (1991). I opened it on the title page. There was an inscription:

> 'To Dominic on the event of your first birthday.
> Designed for bedtime reading, and to keep you glued to your pillows, from the imagination of Kenneth Grahame,
> Toad of Toad Hall, and The Wind in The Willows'.

Susan said, 'What are you doing?' I could only choke, 'Not the books.'

I eventually did bring the box of VHSs and DVDs down and placed it on the kitchen table. Dom was three and a half years old when the animated film, *Toy Story*, was released in the US. *Groundhog Day* was one of his all-time favourite movies, but the 1995 *Toy Story* was without doubt his favourite childhood movie. Buzz Lightyear was also his favourite toy and despite being used and played with every day Buzz lasted for years. Many a Saturday morning I was woken up by Dom and Buzz bouncing on my bed, both shouting in union, 'Buzz Lightyear, to the rescue!' or 'To infinity and beyond!'

In 1995, Prime Minister John Major resigned as leader of the Conservative Party, which triggered a leadership election. Theresa May did the same twenty-eight years later. So, while the rest of the UK was counting the cost of the local and mayoral elections held a few weeks before, Theresa May, Jeremy Corbyn and Tim Farron were out campaigning for the June snap election. France was tearing itself apart too with an election underpinned by racism from both ends of the political spectrum. Following the US election, a stunned country was still coming to terms with Donald Trump. I woke up this morning to find myself with an erection. This isn't unusual for men first thing in the morning, and I hoped the pseudo-homophone with a slight lisp wasn't lost with all the other elections going on, but it did make me smile for a change. I needed to smile. There had been another suicide bombing the previous day, the deadliest in the UK since Helen was killed in the 2005 London bomb. This time it was in Manchester at a pop concert. Twenty-two people, mostly parents and teenagers, were killed as they were leaving the venue. All political parties suspended their election campaigns.

When I woke up, I wasn't thinking about sex, or the elections. I wasn't even thinking about the bombing. It had been on the news constantly for the last twenty-four hours so my brain was numb – just like my body over the last three years. Sex hadn't been on the agenda and there were a number of reasons for this: I couldn't sleep much, Susan was up very early, so there was only a small window of opportunity. I've consumed vast amounts of alcohol since 2013, not to try to help me sleep but to keep me functioning. It killed my desire and need for sex. More important than the technical or primal aspect of making love, emotionally, Susan and I hadn't been on the same page about Dom, so sex just for comfort, not even intimacy or pleasure, seemed inappropriate. Helen MacDonald in *H is for Hawk* took a different view. 'I was ravenous for material, for love, for anything to stop the loss, and my mind had no compunction in attempting to recruit anyone, anything, to assist. In June I fell in love, predictably and devastatingly, with a man who ran a mile when he worked out how broken I was' (p. 17).

## Not Going Anywhere

It's 18 October 2017. We buried Dom four years ago today. I woke up this morning with death and dying as my first thoughts. Strangely, this time it was of old age, not suicide. It was still a very dark thought but was this a step forward? The week before the burial, we went to visit the church to see the place where Dom was going to rest. The vicar was thinking ahead. He had left a gap between where Dom was going to be – shaded by a young beech tree – and the nearest grave. There was space for four more graves. Since then, without discussing the matter, I had selfishly assumed I would be buried next to my oldest son.

When I saw him in his coffin for the first time, he looked like he was resting. The only visible difference from the last time I saw him, alive, was the graze under his chin, now minimised by undertaker makeup. I touched his chest to make sure the nightmare wasn't a huge prank, and mindlessly to see if his heart was still beating. But he was cold, and my gaze kept being drawn continually to his chin. His heart was motionless in his chest. And now, four years on, I imagined and planned a grand theatrical gesture that I'd stolen from a medieval time, a common practice then. But now, more latterly, I associate it with Thomas Hardy and of course the myth surrounding Percy Bysshe Shelley. After Shelley drowned in 1822, Edward Trelawny took a macabre memento at the funeral pyre.

When my time comes and I'm lying in the morgue at the mercy of the pathologist, after I've been examined and they have double checked that I am actually dead and the autopsy is complete, there will be a set of further instructions. I haven't thought this request through fully yet. For example, I don't think it's something that I need to request in a last will and testament, but I'll check. The pathologist somewhere, somehow, will have been directed to remove my heart. Perhaps I should consider writing an 'After I'm dead' note? That seems the most sensible. Susan will have a lot of other things to think about. I could make a video and leave it on a memory stick in the same envelope. It might give the impression there was some control or organisation in my life after all.

What would my afterlife guidelines look like?

1. Remove heart.

2. Music that should be playing when guests arrive at the church – *Virginia Plain*: Roxy Music (1972).

3. Music that should be playing when guests leave the church – *Sex Machine*: James Brown (1970).

4. Funeral tea: Taylor's sixty-year Port, with Stilton cheese, McVities Digestives, fruit loaf, honey and Carr's Water Biscuits. (Possibly relax this to a full cheese board if Susan insists. She only likes Stilton stuffed in Portobello mushrooms baked with garlic)

5. At some point at the church or the wake – Reuben can choose the time – put on full blast *Back to Life, Back to Reality*: Soul II Soul (2009). That'll give everyone something to dance to. It's a start, but probably needs a bit more thought.

Whilst the pathologist is rummaging around in there, they can take anything else in good condition for organ donation. Slim pickings, I suspect. My heart, embalmed, would be placed in a small casket, and at my interment it would be buried with Dom, in his place. And then my body could finally be rested in the reserved space by his side. We would both be waiting for Susan to join us, perhaps on his other side? I have assumed it would be me next; I'm sixty in seven weeks and Susan is as fit as a butcher's dog. She walks six or seven miles through Greystoke Forest every day with Lucy, Dom's collie, and Kadie, her dachshund.

I think about Dom lying in his coffin, encased in wood, surrounded with lace and padding, and silence. I wish with all my will that he'd had the padding around him that night, or at least the cotton wool we used as parents in the early years. I imagine myself there now, lying in my casket on the morning of my interment, just as I remember he was, eyes closed, arms folded across his chest. Typing now in bed I suddenly become claustrophobic when I imagine the lid being placed above me. I have to move and make some coffee to shake it off. Could I live the rest of my death in a six by two box? Lucy is nearly six, and her eyes seem to be holding out. If she lives to a good age, I'll be sixty-seven or sixty-eight. It dawns on me that our next canine companion is likely to outlive me. On balance, would it be more acceptable in today's world of political correctness, to leave my heart where it is, and to ask instead for the vet to remove Lucy's heart when she dies, and place that at Dominic's feet in a small heart shaped casket? After all, Lucy was his faithful companion, even if it was just for a short while.

# Part 2 - Oscillation and Confrontation

# Saturday, 17 March 2018 – Beech House

So, we're here, our new house. Just the two of us.

# Tuesday 25 December 2018 - Beech House – 5.45am

There will be millions of children lying awake or just starting to wake up as I write these words. Excited, bursting with anticipation of what they will find under the tree when they go downstairs. Over the weeks and months leading up to today, countless lists will have been written, one by the children asking Santa for all their wishes and dreams, and another by mum or dad, preparing a 'to do' list for the perfect day. What groceries will be required? Shall we order a fresh turkey or buy a frozen one? Does everyone like prawns? Note to self: Don't forget to put the cranberry sauce on the table because you forgot to last year, and importantly, get the spare chairs out of the garage in plenty of time to dust them down. These are the principal, weighty issues, just for this one day.

    The TV is on in the background, an advert is running. The camera pans into a family of six people sat around a roaring fire, there's a twinkling tree in the background, a lazy sausage dog in the foreground, and falling snow through a window to the right. They're unwrapping Christmas presents, smiling, having a wonderful seasonal moment together. Suddenly, the scene comes to life with a multitude of green screen and cartoon graphics. The Afro-Caribbean grandfather figure morphs into a lean, mean lycra superhero, who chases and stops a runaway train saving millions of people. Little Johnnie of non-specific ethnicity or obvious gender (so he could be Janie) beams with pride at his hero and captures the whole incident on his/her new HD,1000 mega-pixel phone camera, which incidentally, also has the ability to switch on the central heating from the jungle/arctic circle or driving home from work, at the same time it can play Dad's favourite song when Johnnie/Janie heads off to uni and is feeling low. A well-known American actor voices over 'Only £699 with unlimited data, order yours now'. Sold, to the electronic cigarette smoking single mother of four, who goes to the food bank every month.

It's Christmas morning, millions of excited kids didn't sleep much last night and are desperate to sneak next door and bounce on mum and dad's bed begging to go downstairs to see what Santa has brought them. The weeks of preparation and build-up to this one day is over, the adults have done all they can to make it the most memorable family day and the most perfect, enjoyable day of the year. They just want everyone to enjoy the atmosphere and appreciate the time with close family and good friends.

In reality, all the adults are stressed. They've over spent and will still be paying for Christmas in July. They've over prepared. The hype, starting at the end of September and builds into a frenzy to the point where; you HAVE to buy that final jar of pickled walnuts on Christmas Eve, just in case. (There's one still in the cupboard from last year). You need to buy 2 kilos of sprouts, just in case, but no one really likes them. On the day you buy the tree (now the 1$^{st}$ December) you have to buy another set of 250 soft white lights, with 12 flashing modes. Just in case.

Why am I being such a miserable and cynical old bastard on Christmas morning? I can't help thinking of how it used to be…

# Christmas 2010, Vicargate

Overnight, the smell of cooking turkey had slowly drifted upstairs. It's the Loftus traditional Christmas morning wake-up call. The bird has been in the bottom oven of the Aga since 11 pm, Christmas Eve. It will be cooked to perfection when the tinfoil is removed and it's browned off in the top oven. Downstairs, the smell of pine needles and cherry wood logs smouldering on the fire blend with the turkey essence to set the perfect aromatic ambience for the perfect Christmas morning.

I didn't need to peep through the bedroom blinds to see if it had been snowing. There's been a five or six inch covering for days. Snowmen have been built, and the kids have already sledged and snowboarded down the hill from the house to the beck that runs between us and the nearest farm, Well House. Ollie Strong lives there, one of Dom's best friends. It's pitch black, and there's no street lighting at Castle Sowerby, but, on a cloudless Christmas Eve like last night, the clear moon and the millions of stars gave a soft cinematic sheen to the ground snow. Lightheaded after I'd put the turkey in the oven, I took my glass of single malt outside. It was minus three degrees, but I sat on the sandstone bench in the orchard. The moonlight transformed each snow-covered tree into a crystal chandelier that reflected its glass secrets like a whisky highball left in the dining room candlelight last night.

As they went to bed carrying their pillowcases, the kids left a mince pie and damson gin for Santa, and a carrot for Rudolph. Reuben had carefully placed them on the hearth next to the log fire, but the dog had eaten the mince pie even before he left the room. As they settled in bed, thinking their private seasonal thoughts, Susan and I quietly brought the boxes of wrapped gifts down from the spare bedroom. Eventually, when the kids were asleep, we stuffed their pillowcases with stocking fillers, and their 'big' presents would be left around the tree and added to the ones that had been dropped off by family and friends over the last few days.

The gift opening was getting progressively later in the morning; Dominic would be twenty in a few weeks, Chloe was sixteen, and Reuben was thirteen a few days ago. It didn't seem that long ago that all three of them would burst into our bedroom carrying their pillowcases at 4 or 5 am. On Christmas morning as all five of us sat happily on our bed, in anticipation of what was under the wrapping paper, I recorded hours of laughing and paper tearing on the VHS video camera. In 2014, I got six or seven of these tapes, which also included footage of family holidays, parties at Vicargate, weddings and Christenings, transferred onto DVDs. As I write now on 25 December 2018, I still haven't had the courage to watch any of them. Nonetheless, on Christmas morning 2010, all of our children now in their teens, the expectation of giving and receiving, and spending the day together, was still very much a part of our family Christmas.

We all came downstairs together. The kettle whistled on the Aga. There was a quick rake of the fire; dry kindling was carefully placed on the still glowing embers. An hour later, there was a pile of unwrapped gifts around the feet of everyone, the living room carpet was camouflaged by torn wrapping paper, and without exception, everyone said, 'Just what I wanted'. Pan into a family of six people sitting around a roaring fire (Linzi was now living at Vicargate); there's a twinkling tree in the background, a lazy whippet in the foreground and as close to the fire as she can get. The dog's back is singed brown from lying next to the fire over the years. There's falling snow through French windows to the right.

So, on Christmas morning 2018, why am I so miserable, apart from the obvious reason that Dominic would be twenty-eight in a few weeks' time. He's no longer a part of that once familiar family Christmas scene. In fact, that scene hasn't happened for the last five years because of his death. Outside the Loftus family, life has gone on without him. All his friends' lives go on as they and their parents had dreamed of on similar family Christmas mornings, as we did.

This year, we have watched from the side-lines as one of Dom's friends bought a house and got married. Another fell in love and he and his girlfriend worked for months on their house, the other boys helping out where they could. Another became the proud father of a baby boy and moved into their new family home with his girlfriend. We have read much of this on social media. We are delighted that they and their parents have been privileged to progress through life as planned. We all know, however, that Facebook only records happy times, and few people post about the unhappy or bad times.

# March 2019

We've been at Beech House for twelve months now. Two years ago, we sold Vicargate, our family home of thirty years, and moved into Dom's empty flat above the Sportsmans. I had an office there anyway with a separate entrance so I could go in and out without disturbing him. I'd only been back once since he'd died to remove all the business-related documentation. Living in his flat was a nightmare. We had no choice. We had nowhere else to go but we were determined to sell the pubs. They had been on the market for three years and last year they were finally sold within a month of each other. We were very grateful to leave Dom's flat behind, but we couldn't rent private accommodation. We had Lucy and Kadie. Landlords don't like dogs. We moved into Susan's brother's house for a few months before moving here.

Dom and I worked together at the Sportsmans, which are some of my dearest and fondest memories. However, my happiest memories of Dom are in and around Vicargate, our forever home. He spent most of his life there, and it gave him an idyllic childhood and easy access to the fells and the lakes as he grew up. When he lived at the Sportsmans, he was its heart and soul and was deeply involved in the family business. Working alongside him also provided some of the proudest moments of my life. He had made and was involved in the best of those memories. After his death, the very existence of Vicargate and the restaurants now provided the worst.

The sale of our old life was partly so we could get on with the rest of our lives. It was a way to try to move on after Dom's death, to let go. It was also partially because we couldn't afford it – I'd not worked properly for almost three years – and sadly, it would have been the appropriate time for Susan and me to go our separate ways.

Today, all the main structural work at Beech House is complete. We built a small extension too. The painting and decorating are also finished so we are at the point of unpacking the Vicargate boxes that have been in storage since November 2016. Vicargate was a bigger house, so when we packed to leave in 2016, thirteen full car loads of once prized possessions went to the tip. Five containers, measuring three meters high, four meters deep, and four meters wide, still went into storage. We also managed to fill Nicola and Gus's garage, and brother-in-law Stuart's loft space.

After Dom's death and packing for the move, we could have taken everything from Vicargate to the tip; nothing was cherished or held importance anymore. I remember reading about Mary Berry, the Aga cook and more latterly a Great British Bake-Off judge. She was a famous avid collector of all things domestic. In 1989, after her son William was killed in a car crash, she said, 'her prized possessions were not prized anymore'. We spend decades striving to buy the things that we think we should own, the items that tell the world who (we think) we are, just simply by their possession. We buy things that stretch us far beyond our budget, generally to impress other people. Posing in front of his Rolls Royce, Ernie Wise reminds us of this folly: 'They are only our 'Aren't I doing well?' possessions.'

We brought the boxes in from the garage one by one, and Susan carefully unwrapped the items. As each Beswick horse, Spode side plate and framed picture was revealed, they reminded us two years later of the contents of our previous life. Next came the dozen 'Aren't I doing well?' Edinburgh crystal glasses and Susan's framed cross-stitch of a dissected onion showing its many layers. It made me think of our life together over the last six years. We've had layer after layer stripped away, each as painful as the last. We got to the point that if the last piece of skin was taken, we would have had nothing. The onion was a proud possession that she'd created when she was eleven years old. She hung it straight away in the new Beech House kitchen. Then came the boxes of family photos. Acres of family photos.

***

I met Chris for a coffee yesterday. We used to work together. I told him we had sold Vicargate and between forced happy memories and as he left the cafe, he told me that he was glad that I was 'moving on'. Move on, I've learned, is a standard placation. Six years later, I've certainly moved. Perhaps it's not on or up but from a position of inertia, darkness and thoughts of suicide. Possibly, that's what Chris meant, so he was half right. Yesterday, though, I had a kind of Julian Assange moment. That moment as he was led out of a room in the Ecuadorian embassy after nearly seven years, blinking, exposed to the world, still pleading his innocence. The world was yet to decide. Still not free, the room in the embassy was exchanged for a smaller one in Belmarsh prison and he was taken there in handcuffs. But now, the discussion about his future can take place, as can the discussion about mine.

Was moving from Vicargate to Beech House also just an exchange to a smaller prison? I've often wondered if I could continue my life in parallel with Dom's death. Can I still live a fulfilling life despite the pain as it burns through my heart when I think about him? I need to feel the hurt and the loss, because if I don't, it might mean I'm forgetting about him, or even worse, by some twisted logic that, by not hurting, his life was wasted. If I'm not grieving for him, then he's gone and I've lost him completely. Can I live with this toragony for the rest of my life so I can keep him with me – at the same time have a life where I can start to enjoy things again? I've had it test me time and time again. I've started to feel relaxed and actually enjoy an ordinary moment: a beer, a feel-good movie or the company of friends. The guilt always descends. But it was something as simple as seeing the sun shine and a butterfly that made me start to think about what moving on meant.

# A Shaft of Light

Susan and I landed at Ngurah Rai, the international airport at Bali. Without telling Susan, I'd arranged with Chloe to meet us there. She took a few days off work and flew in from Darwin. Chloe put a baseball cap on, stood on the other side of the arrivals barrier and pretended to be a taxi driver. She held up a sign with our names on it. It was our thirtieth wedding anniversary and bittersweet.

I woke up in the dark, but instinctively I knew it was a beautiful day. Chloe had gone back to work. Susan was already up and drinking coffee on our terrace in the quiet resort of Rumah. A breeze caught the French window curtains and briefly confirmed my judgement. The room faded back into darkness. I found the gap in the mosquito net and swung my legs out of the bed. I wrapped a bath towel around my waist, opened the curtains and stepped out into the heat, instantly missing the comfort of the air-conditioning.

There wasn't a cloud in the sky and nothing moved in the compound. Susan read in silence. Not a bad-tempered silence – we've experienced lots of those in the last three years. It was an environmental tranquillity: the usually quiet staff were even more invisible; not a bird or insect made a sound. Despite the main road, carrying hundreds of scooters and motorcycles heading into the city, only eight hundred meters away, there was nothing. No recycled water ran back into the swimming pool; the surface was yet to be broken. Susan looked up and smiled, but it was an Orange Gull butterfly that broke the silence. I walked to the edge of the shade. As I left its protection, the brightness of the sun shattered my eardrums. The butterfly briefly settled on a stone statue of Vishnu; the bright yellow markings of the Orange Gull hypnotised me. It rose again and the brown feathering on its hindwings fluttered, resembling a native American headdress. Although it was a tranquil peace, seeing Vishnu and the butterfly momentarily glowing in the sunlight gave me a spiritual peace.

*\*\*\**

The only items still left in the garage are a dozen boxes of books. Mainly Reuben's. We haven't got anywhere to display or keep them. As mentioned earlier, I don't feel comfortable getting rid of books, even if they are given away for someone else to read. The dozens of family photos that we had displayed around Vicargate are now unpacked and appearing on the walls and windowsills of Beech House. I suddenly feel vulnerable. I have to look into Dominic's eyes again. Even in my discomfort, I can't change the past, even if I don't want Susan to display or keep them. It's our family history, our story, displayed around the house like a pictorial Wikileaks. It was Assange's stark photo on the news – his matted hair, long grey beard, his eyes caught in the headlights of the police van – that reminded me of me. Whether he accepts it or not, he's been isolated for too long; whether he's innocent or not, like me, he has to face up to the truth.

\*\*\*

This memoir is only part of Dom's story, little snapshots of the life before and after his death. Dom was twenty-two when he was killed, but his life story began many years before that, even before we bought Vicargate. Moving to Castle Sowerby and having Dom, Reuben and Chloe was always part of the master plan. Although he was born, christened and raised at Castle Sowerby, it is also now his spiritual home and resting place. I promised him a book of memories and this is it. Except the memories are written pictures of moments of his life, and of the life going on around us at the time.

When you walk around someone's house and you see the photos and paintings on the wall, often there's no rhyme or reason to why or how they're displayed. It's just everyday life going on and we try to capture it. A family house generally has richer pickings because of school photos: an individual child, a class or three siblings. We have pictures of all our three children together as they were at infant school at the same time. In the house there are photos or sketches of pets too, or even wild animals like foxes and deer that I'd been lucky enough to photograph around Vicargate. Susan's mum, Judy, bred rough collies like Lassie, and in the kitchen there's a black and white photo of Susan and her brother Stuart, and a show winner called Merry Legs. The photo was taken fifty years ago. Next to it is a photo of Susan and Dom. He's about four weeks old and staring out at me from the living room wall. His head is leaning into his mother's breast; Susan is smiling but he isn't. He's just staring ahead. It's haunting and reminds me of a photo I saw in a Jewish Museum in Budapest. It was a Second World War photo, a sad scene of Jewish men standing behind a barbed wire fence. There's a melancholy, a resigned look, emaciated people in striped clothing who seem to have accepted their fate.

*if only ya could see into the future, ehh dad?*
*wud u and mam still have had me if you new?*

# 10–18 October 2019 – Polo's Treasure, Venice

In the reducing light, the tourists on the east bank of the Rio de S. Casson were struggling with their tourist maps. 'The smart ones use Google Maps,' I said to Susan, just as my phone signal dropped to no reception. As we pulled our suitcases behind us through the market, even though the traders had left hours ago, there was still a profound smell of fish. The noses of the local cats systematically swept the floors underneath the empty stalls, not willing to miss a single scale.

Despite no phone signal, we eventually found Polo's Treasure and left our bags in the bedroom. We were joining some friends the next morning on board the Silver Shadow, but that night, in contrast, we paid €4 for a small table at the Cantina do Mori to enjoy some bread, local sparkling wine and seafood risotto. At the end of this week six years ago, we buried Dominic. I shared twenty-two years with him. Three months short of twenty-three years, to be precise. Three months is a precious amount of time in the final scheme of what time we had. I often reflect on the concept and the meaning of time. It's a level of grief that many people go through, regretting the lack of time we had with them, or not spending or devoting enough time when they were alive. I expected much longer. I had imagined babysitting grandchildren, reading passages from Wind in the Willows to them from the hardback book I bought their father and read when he was their age.

After dinner and back at Polo's Treasure, I opened the windows and we sipped wine in bed. Susan fell asleep quickly and, with my Kindle balanced on my chest, I started to read. Julian Barnes's book *Levels of Life* (2014) was the only light in the dark room. Even the street noise was diminished. I started to realise that other authors can offer different dimensions to my sense of grieving. Barnes's book for example, is a testimony to his love for his wife. He creates vivid pictures for us about early photography, and adventurous men moving around the world in hot air balloons. Captain Fred Burnaby, the primary protagonist, is hot air ballooning over France or crossing the English

Channel at every opportunity. I have this image of an airborne explorer, an English gentleman in a gentle and kind wind, smoking a 'dangerous' cigar and acting like an English gentleman would do as if he was on the lawn of a country house having a picnic. A bit like Shackleton in his brogues, but at a thousand feet, and without the croquet mallet. The crossings are not like that – they're very dangerous; you are at the mercy of the weather and where it takes you. The balloon itself is fragile and combustible, and the take-offs and landings are more luck than judgement. This, however, is a clear metaphor for Barnes's journey through his grief, and we keep riding that balloon horizontally and vertically however scared we are, but at least with 360-degree visibility in the cockpit of our surroundings, even if we have no control of the direction of flight. This ability to see where we've been and what lies ahead, even if strong forces are stopping us getting there sometimes, is the reason why I write about Dominic.

On page eighty-five, Barnes discusses patterns. One of the patterns he focuses on is broken legs. Several of the characters, both historical and fictional, break their legs. This includes his wife in Chapter Three, who fell down the steps outside their home. Before his wife's death he may just have considered these a bizarre coincidence. He believes that, as humans, we need patterns or routines but grief destroys all patterns and more. To survive we need to reconstruct new patterns as we reconstruct our lives. More importantly, as writers, we believe that the patterns of our words add up to our stories, ideas and our truth whether we are grieving or not; this is our raison d'être. This might be true, and I'm glad I'm a writer, and not a postman, a bus driver or a landscape gardener. But I ask, how can we be so removed and dispassionate that we can write about the death of our child? As a writer, I find that space. I'm an autoethnographer for a few hours each time I write.

Like CS Lewis, Julian Barnes wrote *Levels of Life* (2014) following the death of his wife. Pat had been married before; her first husband took a long time to die of cancer, and so in preparation for her death, she asked Barnes in advance for a reading list, and he 'assembled the classic texts of bereavement' (p. 69). I don't know what the books were – he didn't say –but he had time to gather them together. 'But they made no difference when the moment came' (p.69). When Susan and Chloe cleared Dom's apartment, he only had three books on his bookshelf and they were all about dog training. His book *Wind in the Willows* has always sat on my bookshelf. I often ask myself, did Dom or Linzi buy the three books together when they got Lucy? Did he actually read them? Did he miss Vicargate? Was he happy in that apartment on his own after Linzi left?

*Levels of Life* is split into three sections: namely, a brief history of nineteenth-century Anglo-French ballooning, with the pioneer of aerial photography – Gaspard-Félix Tournachon (aka Nadar). Also, in part one is another pioneering balloonist, colonel Fred Burnaby, and the French actor Sarah Bernhardt. The second part is a fictional narrative based on Burnaby and Bernhardt; 'We may establish they met', Barnes writes, as he brings them romantically together. The final section is a fifty-five-page essay about Pat and his reaction to her death. Whilst the first two sections portray aeronautical life and relationships on the ground, the final section describes descent, darkness and despair. Nothing had prepared Barnes for Pat's death, not even his own parents' deaths, nor all the thinking about death that went into his book that had been published only a few months earlier, *Nothing to Be Frightened Of* (2008). Nothing helped him to cope with the loss.

The extended metaphor of hot air balloons and photography runs in and out of all three sections and ultimately, the title pulls it all together in as far as, in life, we can soar as high as a balloon when in love, or we can hit the ground hard in grief, and everything in-between. Even though it reads as three different books, he still manages to capture the phenomenology of traumatic loss within its slim chapters.

I found myself questioning the different ways in which Barnes explains his grief and what I could learn from it. If I were to survive the multiple ways that Dom's death tore me apart, how might I draw upon a diversity of ideas as Barnes does, but in a way that fully represents the multiplicity of experiences I'd shared with Dom? Initially it was with Barnes's frankness about his emotions that I drew parallels with my own feeling at the time. There were several incidents and writers that pulled me from the brink more than once. Barnes was one of those writers. He seemed to encapsulate everything that grief does to a person. They are possessed by the dead. They are haunted by them. The living become literary archives dedicated to the dead. Until they die themselves, they are bound to keep the dead alive within them. As Barnes wrote:

> …but I was her principal rememberer. If she was anywhere, she was within me, internalised. This was normal. And it was equally normal – and irrefutable – that I could not kill myself because then I would be killing her. She would die a second time, my lustrous memories of her fading as the bathwater turned red. (p. 90)

Reading a paragraph on page eighty-nine of *Levels of Life* reinforced my thoughts about staying alive. Barnes admits that he couldn't allow himself to commit suicide because if he did, he would also be killing Pat again. Barnes writes (p. 109) that he was also worried that he could only remember a certain period of their life together. He says that although the memories come back, he is worried that these memories are not the same memories, and his wife isn't there to corroborate them. I'm lucky: I have Susan to remind me should I forget or remember incorrectly.

We had left the Venice hotel and were on board the Silver Shadow the next night. I tried not to scratch the dozen mosquito bites on my arms and back. I suspected it was the work of a stealthy flying assassin on Calle del Campanile that came unseen through the open window and into our unlit room. Each puncture wound had swollen dramatically and become irritable and self-contained. The next morning, I brushed my teeth and as the toothpaste dribbled down my chin, I realised my top lip was numb. The feeling was like I'd been to the dentist for a filling and had an injection. There was no evidence of a bite near my mouth. I mentioned it to Susan at breakfast as I tried to stop the coffee escaping my mouth.

'Perhaps you've had a stroke?' she joked.

'Perhaps,' I replied, 'Is my smile straight?'

I smiled falsely; in fact, it was more like just showing her my teeth as my face was now numb. I couldn't feel my teeth either. She confirmed there was a droop on the left-hand side of my face.

We went up to the pool deck for lunch and then up a further deck to watch the cast off and admire the coastline as we quietly sailed through the channel and out into the Adriatic. Venice city centre was on our port side and Lido di Venezia on the starboard. We passed a public water taxi going in the other direction, and a solitary male passenger waved and smiled a genuine happy smile. I wondered who he was and where he was going? Dom was always 'Smiler' to me. Not only did he have the most engaging smile; it was constant. I can imagine that it could have been him waving from that water taxi; it's something he would have done, even at the age of twenty-nine, which he would have been in just over three months' time.

## Croatia

We had an early start this morning and went to visit the national park just outside the port of Split, the Adriatic gateway to Croatia. The last time we were here, it was called Yugoslavia. Despite the war and death of tens of thousands of people, it's still a beautiful coast line. We were in a group of seventeen and at the younger end of the procession that slowly shuffled across the wooden raised walkways. We snaked in and out of the waterfalls and trees following the boardwalk, our local guide constantly talked about the main features of the landscape, often saying in her almost Prussian lilt that made everything sound like an order not a request, 'Please tell me if I'm walking too fast.' I did think that we couldn't walk any slower if we tried, but there were some older people to consider.

Several walked bowlegged, but most walked like they'd had an accident in their pants, and I wondered if it was a precursor to getting old, going back to the beginning, resembling a baby ready for a nappy change. Many visibly struggled at various points especially if it involved steps. We got to the end of the walk and sat down with some coffee and cake. I said to Susan, 'when does a person officially get old?' the coffee dribbling down my chin as my numb lip failed to contain it, but I managed to stem the flow with a napkin.

As we sat, I watched an elderly gentleman in a baseball cap, trainers, a checked shirt, cargo pants and a Gillet with a dozen pockets. Slowly, almost frame by frame he propped his walking stick up against a tree. He produced a phone, held it in landscape mode in both hands and he glacially brought it up to his eye level to take a picture. I hope he had the image stabilization feature activated otherwise none of his holiday snaps will be in focus.

Multi pocketed Gillet man wasn't funny but it was a reality that struck me, and today as I still consider life as we get older, I realised my superhero cover is about to be blown. Something this week has shone a light into my telephone box and exposed a vulnerability. I've been to see the ships doctor twice, and slightly relieved each time that I got the opening hours wrong. But despite the Monty Python classic of 'It's only a flesh wound.' I really need to go back between five and six this afternoon. Not only is my lip still numb, my right eye, my good eye, is red veined and moisture is now constantly building up generating that feeling that you get when a cold wind hits your face unexpectedly. This in turn is blurring my vision. I've googled 'Stroke' and it seems a stroke can also affect a victim's vision.

So, the evidence is stacking up, and if the doctor confirms it later, then my mortality will also be confirmed which I've constantly denied. Not only do I wear my heart on my sleeve, I've always also worn my underpants outside my trousers. I always thought I would live forever, apart from the period when I wanted to kill myself.

I decided to visit the ship's doctor, and while I waited outside her surgery, I started to reflect on Barnes's wife, Pat Kavanagh; she died of a brain tumour at the age of sixty-eight. She had few choices, the illness was too far gone, and probably her age was against her. It seems from his account that she came to accept the outcome and prepared herself for it, including the list of books to buy from Waterstones as she waited for death. Dom, on the other hand, was ninety seconds into a ten-minute journey and was killed instantly. No preparation, no goodbyes and no time to order books from Waterstones. What if he hadn't been killed in the crash? What if he had been badly injured but had permanent brain damage? Or he'd lost one or both of his legs, which happens all the time in car crashes? We'd still have him, and he'd still have us. We'd still be able to touch and talk to him. He'd adapt and we would adapt.

'Have you got white coat syndrome?' the doctor asked.
'I don't know what that is.'
'Your BP is 160 over 105, and hypertension is sometimes caused because patients are anxious about being in hospital.'
'In that case, no. But I am anxious that I can't feel my mouth or my face, and I've got coffee and red wine stains down most of my shirts.'

Dr Joanne Dy, the ship's doctor, gave me some corticosteroids, some aspirins and some choices. Later, as I took my 'one per day, ten minutes before a meal' steroid, I thought again about Dr Dy. She didn't think I'd had a stroke but couldn't rule it out. She also told me that she could book an MRI scan for me when we berthed at Corfu the next day. She told me not to panic; it's more likely Bell's palsy, so I said no. She thought it wasn't linked to the bites either.

When I was younger, because I was constantly bitten, I had a theory. I thought that mosquitoes were attracted to the smell of sex. It's extremely difficult to write that decades later without seeming both arrogant and naïve, but for the sake of accuracy, when we were young, especially when we were on holiday, sex was a firm part of our relationship, and we had lots. At least that's my recollection of it.

I also thought that I was a romantic. I wrote poetry about Susan; I read poetry to her. I whispered in her ear, plagiarising Shelley and Byron. I took her to Paris when she was seventeen and I was twenty-one. We stayed in Pigalle, which I thought was doubly romantic, joking with the hookers on the street corner and then having dinner at the Moulin Rouge. My most romantic gesture of all came after that first holiday. After we made love, I didn't take a shower. I loved to have the smell of her on me until I'd showered again. It reminded me of the last time we touched and only I knew about it. It's also why I thought I was constantly bitten.

> You put together two things that have not been put together before. And the world is changed. People may not notice at the time, but that doesn't matter. The world has been changed nonetheless. (Levels of Life, p. 3)

So, like Barnes, I put two things together. I coupled the pain of swollen bites and a pleasure, which had not been connected before, and we created a secret between us for forty years. In Paris we were two kids. No-one noticed us sitting in the Parisian sunshine on the steps of the Opera Garnier. I accepted being bitten because I wanted to love her. As I sit in our ship's cabin now, thinking about the symptoms of getting old, my arms looking like a range of Pink Himalayas, this theory is now debunked. Unless, of course, mosquitoes can still pick up the smell of sex from months ago.

# Why We Need to Remember

I've written prolifically over the last six years in an effort to give me lucidity or even some direction. As I read Joan Didion's *The Year of Magical Thinking* (2005) I'm offered another view and further clarity on my own position. I'm not talking about the achievement of a zen-like state. I still don't accept Dominic's death, or the ghastly timing of the Greystoke Forest stoat. I never will. Yet, by acknowledging that dying is part of life's cycle, as Didion discovered, there is an inevitability and an opportunity. It's our instinct to stay alive, to protect our offspring in order to continue our DNA and our biological legacy.

In his book *The Consolations of Philosophy*, Alain De Botton (2014) writes about Epicurus (341–270 BC) in an essay, 'Happiness, an Epicurean acquisition list' (p. 56), and explains his philosophy on how we can live happier lives. It's a short list of three things: Friendship, Freedom and Thought. De Botton quotes Epicurus as saying, 'There are fewer remedies for anxiety than thought. In writing a problem down or airing it in conversation, we let its essential aspects emerge. And by knowing its character, we remove, if not the problem itself, then its secondary, aggravating characteristics: confusion, displacement, surprise' (p. 58). In my case, I decided to write it all down to tell the world about Dominic and our journey together. But either way the process is near completion, the narrative is being written, his after-life story and mine are now being bound together digitally.

Like most young people, Dom's life was always out there digitally for all to see. I found a picture of him just recently on Facebook. It was one taken during the lads' first outing in the 'Glendale', the camper van that they'd renovated between them. Dom did the electrics.

This photo was taken at Derwentwater, opposite Surprise View in the summer of 2013.

In Didion's book *The Year of Magical Thinking* (2015), she too has assured the memory of her husband, John. She writes about his life as well as his death, keeping him in her everyday conversations and in the conversations that she has in her head. 'I remember thinking that I needed to discuss this with John' (p. 15), she wrote after his death. I do that even today. For a long time, as I was walking or driving and I thought of something or I saw something that I thought Dom would be interested in or would have a view on, my finger automatically went to the shortcut key on my phone to call him. Then of course, finger paused, eyelids close. The anger is palpable.

In a similar vein to Lewis and Barnes, Joan Didion struggled with why, as writers, we need to write about and remember our loved ones. In *The Year of Magical Thinking* (2005) she wrote, 'I know why we try to keep the dead alive: we try to keep them alive in order to keep them with us' (p. 225).

Whilst it took Barnes five years to write and publish Levels of Life, Joan Didion wrote *The Year of Magical Thinking* (2005) in just twelve months. It's the story of the aftermath following the unexpected death of her husband, the writer John Gregory Dunne. In all the grief theories I'd researched, the common denominator, particularly in prolonged grief, was the steps, stages or tasks the griever has to go through to form some sort of a resolution. I was curious about why Didion picked such a short time frame and of course I wondered about the title. There is absolutely nothing magical about losing someone, especially in Didion's situation. She was married to Dunne for over forty years; at the same time that John died, her daughter Quintana was gravely ill. At some point after his death, Quintana shows signs of improvement and Didion starts to think positively about her daughter's wellbeing and eventual recovery. This is calming to Didion, and like Chloe, Dom's sister, she imagines that John is still alive but living somewhere else. On that basis, she leaves all his possessions where they are, just in case he comes back and 'needs a pair of shoes'. Shuchter and Zisook (1988) describe this as 'continuing bonds.' They ran seminal studies in San Diego and discovered that some widows could maintain this sense of their loved ones for years; Didion did eventually realise that this way of thinking (magical) is a fallacy and John won't be coming back.

The main thing that was holding Didion back was guilt. She felt that she could have done more to save John. He'd had a massive heart attack during dinner. She didn't know, but he was already dead when she looked at him across the table. I also felt this burden on me even though I wasn't there when Dom died. I too was at the dinner table when he was killed, and that guilt still haunts me as I write this. The last few weeks, months, years before the death constantly play out in my head. I look for things I could have done differently that might have saved his life. It wasn't until Didion read the stark coroner's report that she realised that there wasn't anything she could have done differently that would have made a difference. To date, April 2021, I still haven't seen Dom's report, but I still fret about what I could have done to save his life.

Didion witnessed the fragility of life but demonstrated our resilience to continue. We continue to carry these ghosts with us. We are changed by keeping them close to our hearts. She said, 'Leis go brown, tectonic plates shift, deep currents move, islands vanish, rooms get forgotten' (p. 227). The game changer for Didion was realising that she could write and publish her book without her husband's support. So ultimately, even though it could be painful at times, she could still exist without him. At this point, I can see her striving to get to Worden's third task (*Grief Counselling and Grief Therapy*, 2011), which, after accepting the reality and processing the pain, is adjusting to a life without someone's physical presence. The conclusion doesn't provide the reader with a sense of closure. While Didion decides to go 'with the flow', she also suggests that the novel has only documented one phase of the grief process, and that while her (temporary) insanity has subsided, no clarity has taken its place. As the title of her book illustrates, Didion has limited her discussion to a single year. It's important to note, however, just how far Didion has come in that year, but I think I can recognise that, like me, she has yet to experience full emotional resolution and still needs to create a new connection with John in her memory. The memoir ends as she remembers swimming with John, who gives her advice to go with the flow of the tide and the waves as they exit a beach cave. She decides to take that advice and try to get on with her life without him.

# Dealing with Death

Despite how conditioned we are culturally, as a western society, we are ill prepared for death, especially an early or unexpected one. Consequently, we are ill prepared for its aftermaths of loss, grief, bereavement, and ultimately deciding which is the next door to go through. This is a complex matter, and is influenced by many things, including our religion, our societal and cultural beliefs.

We talk about death and dying in almost the same way we talk about winning the lottery over dinner. 'What would you do with €170 million if you won EuroMillions?' The after-dinner talk about death may also go…

'Blimey, did you read about that young boy who was killed on the Greystoke Road? The driver was pissed and the police say he was driving at 120 miles an hour – what a way to go! If you had a choice, how would you want to die?'

And we all say,

'Oh God, imagine drowning, burning to death, falling off a building, being eaten by sharks...?'

'Probably in my sleep.'

But, like winning the lottery, losing someone always happens to someone else.

Would it help us handle grief better if we discussed the meaning of death earlier on in life? That's an easy question for me to ask as I'm on a 90-degree learning curve as I write. As touched on earlier, there are many gates and passages that we travel through, sometimes so quickly that we don't even acknowledge the gatekeeper or the transition. It's accepted as part of the life cycle. As a society some of the gates we pass through are planned for and celebrated as a 'special' stage of life, depending on our religion and culture. Things like birth and marriage are universal. Other stages, like our body developing as we get older, are often not discussed. In many societies, for example, puberty can be a mystery. Suddenly we have stomach pains and periods, or we find hair growing under our arms, and no-one told us – officially – it was going to happen. As all this is going on, chemicals like testosterone are charging around inside us, we receive an internal memo about deodorant and the next thing we know, we are looking for a suitable mate.

It could be argued that it's our responsibility as parents to prepare our children for things like puberty and the general navigation through life. Equally then, should we prepare or protect our children from the stark reality that faces everyone on the planet, death? I never gave a thought to discussing dying with Dom. He still had lots of life stages or doors to open before thinking about it. As parents, we teach them that they're special, that they can achieve anything they set their mind to, and there are no limits to their abilities. And, as we did with all our children, we taught Dom about love and respect. As parents we should teach these things, but not to the exclusion of the real consequences of starting this journey through life, which is ultimately death. Does religion lead us into a false sense of security about dying with the promise of a life after death? Christianity offers us the ultimate step through the final door, the pearly gates, for the good and the meek, which for Christians, is seen as the final path.

*\*\*\**

Dr Shelley Carson, psychology lecturer at Harvard University, notes that 'Losing someone you love certainly offers a writer the opportunity for crafting a personal and creative narrative.' It can be difficult to translate that into a real-life scenario, especially when you are the loser. Dom is the real loser, but by writing about him, perhaps I can turn him into a winner? He isn't here to defend himself or corroborate my story, but creativity doesn't give a toss. Carson goes on to say that there are two types of creativity – 'innovative creativity' and 'expressive creativity' – and adds that 'innovative creativity is best suited to problem-solving, while expressive creativity can use negative energy and channel it into creative work as a means to assist with loss or trauma.' Furthermore, 'loss and creativity are two essential parts of the human experience, and when we experience loss, creativity might just be the best way out' (Cerebral Cortex magazine, Volume 26, 2016).

I have an ethical and moral problem too at this point. Would Dom want me to write about him? If he was here, I have a nagging thought that he would be embarrassed. Also, if I do write something, will it be powerful enough to reflect his life and how I feel about him losing it? The psychologist Henry Seiden not only echoes Carson's view; he suggests that 'creativity is the essential response to grief' ('Silent Grief', 2007). Does he mean that we don't need permission to write about the dead? Nevertheless, Seiden's findings resonate with my own experience over the last few years. I sank deeper into depression after finally admitting to myself there was no afterlife, certainly not one I could find. I found some consolation as I read other writers' accounts of their grieving experience, and even more so when I started to write about it myself. At this juncture, if you start to write you can use it to explore your own grief. This also rings true in the grief works of other authors I've read, such as McDonald, Didion and Barnes. Albeit creatively and in different ways, they directly address their psychological landscape after the loss of someone they loved.

As I started to look for links with grief and depression, it was interesting to note that any other emotion we feel and react to, such as sadness or joy, also causes similar chemical reactions in the body. Carson emphasises that when we experience sadness it results in a deactivation of the left prefrontal areas of the brain. The left hemisphere generates positive emotions like joy and hope, whilst the right hemisphere dispenses emotions like anxiety. Unsurprisingly, the right hemisphere is more active during periods of grief. But here's the rub: grieving seems to initiate the partial deactivation of the left hemisphere rather than the over-activation of the right hemisphere. So, even if creativity could help to heal and redirect your life, people don't always feel like tapping into their creative sides following a loss or a major trauma. At the beginning all I wanted to do was write about Dom, and actually getting my thoughts, memories and questions down on the page was more important than grammar, form or narrative arc. It was only later that those things became important.

Carson believes that 'This deep sense of loss requires hard work to fill, and while a person may not feel creatively inclined at first, I see grief (and creative work during periods of grief) as an opportunity' ('How grief and creativity work together', Headspace, p. 5).

She also suggests specific creative activities such as painting, writing or playing music. If you're not a trained musician, she suggests the bongos, noting that drumming is a powerful mood regulator. Painters – amateur or otherwise – need only a blank canvas and paints, and those who write can choose any genre: poetry, a journal or a short story. Carson suggests that if you pick an activity, try to stick with it for three or four consecutive days for twenty minutes per day. She sees this process as a form of performance, that 'Grief provides some of the low notes of our lives that make it a richer symphony overall.'

All of us, at least those of us who are trying to be the 'principal rememberer' (*Levels of Life,* 2014), want to create a full HD, technicoloured, surround sound, 3D life-size image of our lost one in words. This can be an internal, knee jerk reaction over which we have no control. We desperately want to save, rebuild or reinvent the crackling, pixilating hologram fading before our eyes in the shadow of their death. There isn't a 'one size fits all' emotional reaction to the death of someone we know; there are many parameters that affect how we feel, how we react to and handle grief.

# George Orwell, Why I Write (1946)

It's Christmas 2019 and I'm home alone. At this point I'm not sure if I'm Macaulay Culkin, or the bumbling burglar Joe Pesci. Susan has gone away with Reuben over Christmas. Chloe has left Sydney to continue her world tour before returning to the UK, so they'll meet her in the Philippines and return mid-January. I've restocked the anorexic wine rack, topped up the drink's cabinet with single malt and port, and consequently reached yet another fork in the road. Do I take the Winston Churchill approach to writing? He drank a bottle of champagne and brandy every day but wrote and published over a million more words than Charles Dickens (Churchill, 5.2 million words, Dickens, 3.8 million). Quality versus quantity is another discussion. Susan isn't here with 'It's a school night!' Do I just empty the wine rack with no purpose as I did for the first few years after Dom died?

For the first time since 2013, I'm at my desk and I ask myself a real question about my future after Dom. How do I want to be remembered as a person, a father, a husband, a friend, and as a writer?

I pour a (small-ish) glass of Saint-Émilion and start to re-read Walter's paper 'New Models of Bereavement'. As usual, I involve and extend that thought to Dom. Walter's paper is about discussing our memories of the dead, and how we place them in the context of our current lives. I think about that often while the family's away over the festive season. I agree with Walters when he suggests that survivors want to talk about the deceased, typically with other people who knew them. Together they construct a story that places the dead within their lives, a story that they can remember and share. What he means by this is that, unknowingly, we start to write a biography of the deceased that enables the living to integrate the memory of the dead into their ongoing and future lives.

Susan has been away for two and a half weeks now but I've only written two and a half thousand words, hardly Churchillian. This is not because I've drunk a bottle of champagne and brandy every day but because I've done more editing and more reading than writing. Just before they went away, Reuben gave me a slim volume of one hundred pages called *Why I Write*, (1946) by George Orwell. In the book, Orwell is brutal but incisive with his views on British society at the time, and although it was written and published in 1946, much of it is still true over seventy years later. At the start of the book, Orwell gives some of his own backstory, such as working in Burma for the Police Department in 1922 – which influenced his first novel, *Burmese Days* (1934) – he felt he couldn't discuss a writer's motivation to write, particularly his, without knowing something of their early development.

He suggests there are four motives – outside of earning a living – for writing, and they exist in every writer in varying degrees. Most interestingly, he goes on to suggest that the proportions will differ from time to time, according to the situation or atmosphere that the writer is currently in. The four motives are:

- Sheer egoism.
- Aesthetic enthusiasm.
- Historical impulse.
- Political purpose.

I start to unpick the meaning of the four motives and compare them against what has driven me to write about Dom. Orwell explains that the writer's subject matter will be 'determined by the age he or she lives in'. All his six novels were published between 1934 and 1949, and his three non-fiction works, between 1933 and 1938, which was clearly a tumultuous and revolutionary age to live through. He wasn't a well man for most of that period, and whilst he went to Spain in 1938 to sympathise with Catalonia during the Spanish Civil War and was shot by a sniper, he avoided serving in the Second World War due to ill health.

Orwell believed the first three motives are stronger in him than the fourth, but what did he think that the motives mean and how might they affect the writer? He goes on to explain that egoism is often about the desire to seem clever, to be talked about or to be remembered after death. I found this the most interesting. I wrote earlier that the reader might think I'm narcissistic in what I'm doing. I should be grieving about Dominic, not writing about how I feel. I am grieving about him and for me this is the most appropriate way to do so. My motivation is for Dom to be remembered after his death, and consequently because I'm the author, I should be remembered too. Orwell believes that egoism isn't just a writer's motivation: it's also shared with scientists, politicians, artists, lawyers, soldiers and successful business people. Which might explain why Churchill was so prolific. He goes on to say that most people are not selfish, and, after a certain age, even the groups of people mentioned in the last few lines do become philanthropic, care more about others than they do of themselves and give back to society. There is, however, a minority of gifted people who want to live their own lives to the end, and some writers belong to this group.

Orwell goes on to discuss aesthetic enthusiasm: in this context, the perception and appreciation of beauty in the external world. Much of his opinion is centred around the beauty and the use of words, how they are put together, how they sound, the impact on one another, the use of space such as margins, and even fonts. The main point he makes about aesthetic enthusiasm is, as a writer, the desire to share a valuable experience (with a reader) ought not to be missed. This is reflected in his research and also his non-fiction books: *Down and Out in Paris and London* (1933), *The Road to Wigan Pier* (1937) and *Homage to Catalonia* (1938).

The third motive he describes is historical impulse, which he sees as the desire to see things as they are, to get to the facts and record them for posterity. And again, his three non-fiction books reflect this, as do his actions in researching them. For some time, he used to pretend he was a down and out and would sleep in doss houses to try and get the true feeling of being poor. He went to Spain so he could understand the reality of the Catalonian struggle and write about it meaningfully. Of all Orwell's motives, historical impulse might be the biggest driver for the writers of grief memoir. We simply want to record the death of our loved one truthfully for posterity.

Always in the back of my mind is Dom's life and what he meant to his family and friends. How do I position his life digitally, or even now as part of my life? As I flicked through my Kindle heading back to Orwell, I scrolled past George Saunders's novel *Lincoln in the Bardo* (2017). It's a fictional tale wrapped around the death of President Lincoln's son Willie, in February 1862, and the President's struggle with his grief. The story unfolds over one night as Saunders blends historical events through the fiction. The historical facts are well known to us, so we can anchor the fiction in a time, which gives it depth. The meaning of the title, Lincoln in the Bardo, drew me to the book initially during my research on the afterlife. In Tibetan Buddhism, bardo is a transitional state, between death and rebirth into the next life. Willie Lincoln is in the bardo, but Abraham Lincoln is in a transitional state too, grieving for his son while at the same time leading his country during an unpopular civil war.

When I visit Dom's grave, I can't help but think of him six feet below me. I touch the grey head stone as I talk to him, but I know I can't touch his flesh again. I envy President Lincoln as seen through Saunders's eyes. He sits in the mausoleum that night, holding his son whilst he grapples with his death and with the mounting deaths of the Civil War:

> He is just one. And the weight of it about to kill me. Have exported this grief. Some three thousand times. ... A mountain. Of boys. Someone's boys. Must keep on with it. May not have the heart for it. (p. 179)

Yet he did. Not only did he lead his nation through that war; he also preserved the Union, abolished slavery and modernised the US economy, amongst many other things. I, on the other hand, can't get out of bed some days.

Even though I'm reading Orwell, another reason I linger on *Lincoln in the Bardo* is because of the real images of grief that Saunders creates for the reader. In particular, the internal thoughts of Lincoln and the other one hundred and sixty-six 'dead' people who mourn the death of eleven-year-old Willie. I'd also been through my 'afterlife' search a few years earlier and was fascinated by the bardo. It's a wonderfully narrated piece of work, but compared to the other books I'd read on grief, structurally and narratively it was complex. Even so, despite the constant switching of narrators, I skied those narrative moguls and bumps with Saunders, admiring his skill of connecting them, each telling their own grief story or discussing the Lincoln family grief. The novel is very unusual in its dialogue, with most of it told by the ghosts who reside at the mausoleum. It made me think about how other writers express their grief and tell their stories.

I slide my finger to the left along the Kindle and back to Orwell and to his fourth motivation. Political purpose. For example, to push the world or the audience in a certain direction, or to alter their idea about the society they should strive for. He finishes with the assertion that the idea that art should be separate from politics is itself a political attitude. Later, Orwell reflects that had he been born at a different time, he would have written differently, perhaps using more flowery language.

After I'd finished *Why I Write*, I was intrigued by this social – middle class – democrat Orwell, who was genuinely interested in improving the life chances of the poor working class. I'd read *Animal Farm* (1945) and *1984* (1949) before I was sixteen, and I suspect I joined the young socialist party on the back of reading them. I'd not read any of his other works. I immediately downloaded a gratis copy of *Down and Out in Paris and London* (1933) from the George-Orwell.org website and was struck right from chapter one by his novel-esque approach to autoethnography.

When I examine Orwell's research methods and his literary output, he is undoubtedly an autoethnographer: his studies are reflective as he frequently lived and worked among his study group. How could he begin to write about a social situation until he experienced and understood the subjects' own views of their social situation? Many of his books are overtly political and expose the champagne drinking socialist as romanticising the proletariat, and he goes to extraordinary lengths to do this. For example, in *The Road to Wigan Pier*, he lived among the coal miners and the unemployed in Lancashire and Yorkshire. He even went down the mines to experience the conditions for himself. As discussed earlier, he exposed the drudgery and inactivity of the downtrodden, because like me after Dom's death, he sought the truth.

Even today, a reader can relate to a book such as *Down and Out in Paris and London* with its depictions of the struggles of working people. The Paris part of the novel details the nameless narrator's struggles to find work and then his time as a 'plongeur' or dishwasher in an up-market hotel. Autoethnography has been used as a way of telling a story that invites personal connection (Frank, 2000). I was motivated by Orwell's research dedication, how he searched for accuracy and how he lived the life of his study group, the poor and the down and outs of Paris and London. Particularly, he brought it front and centre to the attention of his middle class and intellectual readership. Inevitably it caused me to think about my own upbringing. I felt the pain of a life without hope again as I once did as a child growing up in the slums of Liverpool.

Those dark days of poverty are never too far from my thoughts anyway, and as a parent I'm grateful that we gave Dom everything I lacked in my childhood. We even spoiled him in some people's eyes. Although he didn't care about money and possessions, he never had to think about when he would eat next or where the money to pay the rent was coming from. It might be grasping at straws to think that he had a happy life because he never had to suffer poverty. Nonetheless, I think about the hope that we had for Dom and the hope that we nurtured in him, and I know from his early years the optimism that he felt.

How do I connect myself with the down and outs in the doss houses of Paris and the flotsam in London? I should start with the jetsam of Liverpool in the late 1960s, an abandoned and forgotten generation that was shipped to places like Skelmersdale and Warrington. As a family, we lived with my grandma. It was a three-bedroom terraced house. One bedroom was so damp it couldn't be used. There was more condensation and black mould on the walls than anaglypta wallpaper, and you couldn't get a piece of cigarette paper between the beds, or between the beds and the walls. From the age of seven I slept in the same bedroom as my mother, step father – who had moved in when I was seven – and a younger brother and sister. We three children slept in a second double bed in the corner of the room. Over the next couple of years, a half-brother was born, who slept in the top drawer of the bedroom cupboard. Within two years a half-sister appeared, who took his place in the drawer. He had been put in the double bed with us other children a month earlier. When I was ten years old, my sister, who was four, was moved out and slept with grandma, leaving just us three boys. Within a few months my step-sister was put in a cot beside my mum's bed. For a while, though, seven of us slept in the same bedroom.

The kitchen was a mysophobian nightmare. It had the feeling of a very damp stone garden shed but with the luxury of a layer of linoleum on top of the concrete floor. It was actually quite a big room but impossible to sit in. Its furniture included a push bike, a single dining chair against a wall, and a sky-blue pantry cupboard with frosted glass doors. A solitary light bulb, without a shade, hung from a discoloured, greasy rose in the centre of the ceiling. There was a coal fireplace but it was never lit. I don't know why, but in hindsight I can only assume that coal was at a premium. A four-ring gas oven was on the opposite wall and was the only source of heat, but luckily it was burning every day. On the left-hand ring there was always a tall dull grey steel bucket on the boil. A large pair of wooden handled tongs balanced on top of it. This was a permanent feature even before the half-siblings came along. The only beauty and hope in the house was when my mother drained and wrung out the contents of the bucket and took me outside. She would proudly peg up a dozen white fluffy babies' nappies on the backyard clothes line. It was always sunny during this activity. I admired my mother for knowing what the weather was going to do on that day.

When I was eleven, my mother was offered a three-bedroom house in Skelmersdale, an overspill estate fifteen miles away. It felt like a county mansion compared to the slums of Liverpool.

*\*\*\**

Over the last few years, I've tried to explore those frenzied moments of wanting to remember the past. Not like the realisations and ruminations above, but those desperate and distorting moments, when your brain is unable to process what you're seeing or feeling. Such as going to identify Dom in the morgue at Carlisle. You never escape those moments. I constantly play his life out in my head, but are they my reconstructed memories of his life, my interpretations of how I want to remember him? The memories, sometimes colour, sometimes black and white or sometimes silent, are mainly of his early life as a small boy and often dreamlike. The last few days leading up to his death are as real as you are reading this. Today is slightly different, though: I can recall them instead of just being bombarded by them. That feeling is like practising a speech the day before the event, reciting the words without using cue cards and without speaking out loud. Except without the pressure of someone sitting on your chest.

# A Sad Dad

'Hello, mate, how are you doing? Follow me.'

I didn't get the chance to reply. I followed the doctor to his consulting room. He gestured to a chair next to his desk. I sat.

'You maybe don't recognise me, but we used to come into the Sportsmans?'

I didn't. 'Yes, of course, nice to see you again.'

'So, mate, what can I do for you? When did you move into the area?'

'I'm a bit worried. Sometimes I can't stay awake and just need to lie down. March.'

'Okay, mate, when did this start? Are you in Temple Sowerby?'

'It's been a while now, and it's at any time of the day. No, Newbiggin.'

'What about sleeping at night? You sold the pubs, then?'

'For the last four years I couldn't sleep; now I can't wake up. Yes. Last year.'

This line of questioning went on for five minutes and we covered a lot of ground, not only about my symptoms but about life after Dom.

'Sorry, Ian, but I think you're depressed.'

'Really?' For once I feel okay. I was starting to forgive myself for smiling.

It was true; I did find myself smiling now, even joking with Susan. I was drinking wine sometimes to enjoy it, not just to get pissed. The thing that remained was the guilt that I'd survived. I'd survived Dom's death and Dom; I've outlived him and it kills me. However, I was smiling again and it was a big step.

'I can write a script and give you some pills? It will help you, honest.'

Depressed? Despite the last five years – thinking I was insane, contemplating suicide, Susan's mam actually committing suicide, my mum dying on the toilet, my relationship with Susan nearly down the toilet, drinking until I couldn't remember, selling the house, selling the businesses, completing my masters and starting a Ph.D. – I'd never thought about depression. I just thought I was a 'Sad Dad' and depression was for losers, people who couldn't cope. Depression always happened to someone else. 'Or,' I thought, 'are grief and depression the same thing?'

I became the 'sad dad' after a ski trip in February 2014, 'the pub landlord who lost his son in a tragic car crash'. This is not how I wanted Dom to be remembered.

'I can start you on a low dose, say 20 milligrams? See how it goes?'

Now I'm depressed that I'm depressed.

'Anything else I can do for you?'

'Actually, yes. I heard there's now a cure for blepharitis?'

***

As we grieve, even if we have little or no understanding of the grieving process, at some point we enter a liminal state, a period of ambiguity and disorientation. In my case, I was caught between the spiritual paths of consolation and desolation. Unlike CS Lewis, this wasn't about questioning my beliefs or whether I was moving away from God; it was something more agonising and primal: it was doubting my belief in good and evil, and the understanding of right and wrong. I've researched about self-expressive writing as a grief therapy; I started to wonder if we can deal with this sort of dilemma through fiction? Certainly, by reading fiction we can leave the grief for a while and disappear into the world someone else has created. But what about reading or writing a fictional story about grief? Historical grief, like Willie Lincoln's story in the bardo, despite the fictional wrap, seemed very real, and I recognised many of Lincoln's emotional outpourings. It made me think of another book I'd read recently.

Max Porter's *Grief is the Thing with Feathers* (2015) is a fictional story about the early death of the narrator's wife. Like me, he is adrift after the loss but with the added responsibility of two young sons. As with Saunders's novel, the story is polyvocal and Porter has several narrators, including the dad, the two boys and a crow who enters their lives after her death. The dialogue and narrative flip between the three.

We know very little of the narrator's wife but it's not important to the story. At the beginning he says, 'Grief felt fourth-dimensional, abstract, faintly familiar. I was cold' (p. 1). He was waiting for something to happen. By page two something does happen; the crow arrives and embeds itself into their thinking and their lives. The crow is there to guide them, but I also think it's there to give them hope. 'Hope is the Thing with Feathers' (1891 –Appendix 7) is a poem written and published by the American poet Emily Dickson. She defines hope as a feathered creature deep inside the human psyche that doesn't stop singing, even in the toughest of situations. We know it's a bird by line seven and Dickson concludes that the 'hope' bird never asks for anything.

Dad is a fictional writer working on his new book called Ted Hughes' *A Crow on the Couch: A Wild Analysis*. It's a study of Ted Hughes's work *Crow* (1970), which Hughes wrote after a long period following the suicide of his then wife, the poet Sylvia Plath, in 1963. Much was written and speculated about their volatile relations since, particularly in the 1970s, so dad says, '...Parenthesis Press [his fictional publisher] hope my book might appeal to everyone sick of Ted & Sylvia archaeology' (p. 36). On the same page he also tells us that just as he starts to write the book, the crow appears, '...sometimes patiently perched on my shoulder advising me.?

In *Crow*, Hughes draws on folk tales, world mythologies and, in particular, trickster mythology. In *Grief is the Thing with Feathers*, Porter describes the crow as an 'unkillable trickster' (Dad, p. 37). Paul Radin, anthropologist and author, in *The Trickster. A Study of American Indian Mythology* (1988), says of the Trickster, 'he became and remained everything to every man-god, animal, human being, hero, buffoon, he who was before good and evil, denier, affirmer, destroyer and creator.' And (in Hughes's work) this captures perfectly Crow's own ambivalent identity.

Consequently, I believe Porter's inspiration of the 'hope' bird as a crow comes from *Crow* (1970); however, I think the inner story and emotion come from Porter's early experience as a six-year-old boy and the death of his father. He expresses this in the foreword he wrote for Denise Riley's book *Time Lived without its Flow* (2011). He tells us about the two children in his book and writes,

> These children were an autobiographical device. I had been trying to find a way of writing about what it was like to lose a parent. (p. 1)

Not all the authors I've read recently wrote their books after experiencing a recent death. Porter and Saunders, whose books seem more poetic than the others, are fiction. *Grief is the Thing with Feathers* seems to be more a poem than a novel anyway, but as narratives they are both whimsical, moving and imaginative at the same time. Nevertheless, all the books in some form or another question the social constructionism of the traditional customs and beliefs of death. I identify with other writers who, when they experience the death of a loved one and have that moment of unreality, question their existence. There isn't a chink of clarity in thought; how can we even start to think beyond our grief? Later, however, questions emerge about the meaning of life, and more importantly we look for reasons to continue with our lives. It's this, our imagination and creativity, that comes to the fore in works such as these.

Even though the death of someone close is shattering, for me and for the majority of the writers of grief memoir, the desire or the compulsion to share an experience is one of the strongest motivators. On the contrary, in her memoir *H is for Hawk*, MacDonald says that '[Loss] happens to everyone. But you feel it alone' (p. 13). More interestingly, MacDonald continues with 'Shocking loss isn't to be shared, no matter how hard you try' I can imagine how raw she was at that point, and I'm sure it would have been too emotional for her to talk about her dad and her feeling about him. Even in normal circumstances it can be difficult to describe how you're feeling about something ordinary. Did she have a shoulder to cry on? She did, but as I wrote earlier, he ran a mile after discovering how damaged she was and unable to talk about her intense emotions. After a loss like a parent, when would it have been the right time for Helen to start opening up about it?

Thankfully she did, and we are all the richer for her memories and honesty. I feel privileged to be able to share her journey. I've thought about her sentence a lot. It was in the same paragraph as 'you feel it alone,' and it's the complete opposite to why I'm writing this book. 'Loss isn't to be shared' (p.13), yet she wrote a Costa prize winner in 2014. What I take from that statement, however, is that it's very difficult to share your loss, simply because we haven't got the language that describes how we feel. Like MacDonald, I bought books on grieving, on loss and bereavement. 'They spilled over my desk in tottering piles' (p. 16), so I could try to find the right words. Sometimes you can't speak anyway, not just because you don't know how you feel, think, or what to do, but because you've never experienced such a profound event before. As Orwell explains in *Why I Write* (1946), 'above the level of railway guide, no book is quite free from aesthetic considerations.'

# December 11th

It's my birthday today. I'm not celebrating. I tidied the new garage instead. Anyone looking in there would think I was the king of DIY. There are neat rows of shelves containing most of the tools any competent DIY-er would die for. The display includes, but isn't limited to, half a dozen tool boxes full of hand planes, electric current testers and satellite signal finders, three or four electric drills with a huge selection of bits in three different attaché boxes, two metal boxes of professional screws of all sizes in brass and steel, five saws with varying capability to saw, spirit levels, and every size and shape of screwdriver and hammer. They are not mine of course; they are Dominic's. In one of the toolboxes, which is mine, there are two fishing knives, with stainless steel 5' blades and matching leather sheaths.

In December 2002 we took the three children to Kakslauttanen igloo village in Ivalo, Finland, just north of the arctic circle. We told them it was where Santa lives. We went with David and Karen, the couple who camped in our paddock for two months after Dom was killed. Dom was now eleven, wearing 'product' in his hair, his floppy fringe gone, and even though he had broken his arm a few weeks earlier, this was a happy time. We took Christmas presents with us, and arranged for Santa to knock on the door, speak with the kids and deliver the gifts.

The day before Santa came, Dom and I followed a local guide deep into the wilderness on skidoos. We stopped by a makeshift wooden tepee in a silent clearing in the forest. In the summer season the Finn was a fisherman, operating in the Norwegian sea, and in the winter, he was a guide. He had his fisherman's knife on his belt and picked up a pine branch. The blade was clearly very sharp as he sliced the wood as thin as paper. It looked like a Spanish lady's fan. We went into the tepee and he lit the shaved wood, Dom couldn't believe his eyes. The fan burst into flames like a tissue and the Finn placed it under a pre-prepared fire, which also ignited quickly. Milk and cocoa were added to a pan over the flames and within a few minutes we were drinking mugs of steaming hot chocolate. Between sips of chocolate, Dom couldn't take his eyes off the fishing knife, until eventually the fisherman allowed him to handle it. Later, back in Kakslauttanen, I found a hunting shop that had almost exactly the same knife and bought one for him and one for me. They went into the suitcase for travelling home.

The next night, we were in the log cabin, the adults drinking glühwein. Through the window I could see Santa pulling his sleigh up the track through the snow. The kids were on the floor playing a game.

'Listen!' I said loudly. 'Can anyone hear sleigh bells?'

'Me, me!' Reuben jumped up; he was four.

'I can't.' Dominic was eleven and sceptical.

'I think I can?' Chloe was seven.

Then we all heard the bells. Dom, holding his arm, sat down on a chair quietly in the corner; he didn't believe.

'It must be Santa!' Reuben ran to open the front door. And it was.

Santa had a sack over his shoulder, and said the Finnish version of 'Ho, Ho!!' as he entered the cabin, kicking the snow off his black boots. We found the big guy in red a comfy chair, and he sat down, fluffing up his real white beard. Despite not being able to speak English, he started to produce presents for everyone (except Karen – David had screwed up). Every present (and there was half a dozen for each of the kids) had the person's name on it. I glanced over to Dom. At this point I could see confusion in his eyes. He wasn't sure what he was seeing. A real sleigh outside covered in snow and bells, a real Santa with a real beard, and Christmas presents with his name on. How did they get here? I don't think he would admit it, but just then, just that one more time, he believed in Santa.

The weekend after we got back to Vicargate, Dom and I found a couple of small branches outside and sat by the log burner with our hunting knives. We wanted to see if we could shave the wood as thin as the Fin had. Fortunately, neither of us was hurt and we kept all our fingers, but as usual, I ended up using firelighters to light the fire.

Today, after tidying the garage, I brought our knives back into the house to clean and oil them. Apart from the dust on their leather sheaths, they were as sharp as the day I bought them in Lapland. I rubbed a little oil on the blades and put them on the kitchen table. I switched on the TV and flicked over to the news.

When knives are being discussed anywhere in the media, it's inevitably about the street crime wave that's hit London over the last twelve months, which now seems to be spilling over into the rest of the UK. Killings in London alone, mainly stabbings, are now over 130 in 2018, a 20% increase over 2017. The programme I tuned into was discussing drill music, suggesting it was the motivator and the reason for the increase in stabbings. The reporter was explaining that most of the stabbings are done by, and to, young people. A number of them are rappers. I'd never heard of 'drill', but even so, I wasn't convinced that it was the whole reason for the increase. Unlike Dom's traditional hip-hop, drill is typified by the lyrics. They have been called dark, violent, even nihilistic. Like traditional rappers, drill rappers tend to speak about their lives in their music, but they want to be more graphic and to violently rage against the anomie they find themselves in. Their mantras are gang warfare, revenge, shootings, death, drugs, guns and knives.

The Danish philosopher Søren Kierkegaard (1813–1855) suggested an (early) form of nihilism, which he called levelling. He saw levelling as the process of suppressing individuality to a point where an individual's uniqueness becomes non-existent and nothing meaningful in one's existence can be established. He wrote:

> Levelling at its maximum is like the stillness of death, where one can hear one's own heartbeat, a stillness like death, into which nothing can penetrate, in which everything sinks, powerless. One person can head a rebellion, but one person cannot head this levelling process, for that would make him a leader and he would avoid being levelled. Each individual can in his little circle participate in this levelling, but it is an abstract process, and levelling is abstraction conquering individuality.

(*The Present Age*, translated by Alexander Dru, 1962, pp. 51–53)

I suspect every generation has felt supressed and disenfranchised by the previous one. I can understand the despair felt by the teenagers today on sink estates that are nothing more than modern ghettos. I was there too in the 1960s in the slums of Liverpool, and there by the grace of God goes Dominic. More latterly, though, music and subcultures can be linked, going back to Mods and Rockers in the 1960s. Even though these two groups liked different genres of music and there was violence between them, it wasn't necessarily linked to the music. The lyrics didn't incite violence like drill does today, although the UK rappers will argue it's not the words. They contest that the violence is driven by the stark economic realities faced by London's low-income youth and marginalised communities. The differences between Mods and Rockers were more likely linked to their lifestyles and life choices. They wore different styles of clothes; Rockers drove motorbikes and Mods drove scooters like Vespas or Lambrettas. Later, the Rockers aspired to a more powerful motorbike, and the Mods bought Mini Coopers.

Drill grew in popularity after Dom's death in 2013, especially in London. Artists started to use easily accessible new platforms like YouTube, which I know Dom watched, to boost their audience. I wonder if he would be listening to it today, what he would have thought about it and if he would have been influenced by it. There is no doubt about drill and the influence it has on street gangs – you only need to connect the dots even from Kierkegaard – but surely this nihilistic behaviour must also be driven by their lack of trust in the political and religious authorities? They are trying, as we did in our youth, to place their trust in the individual.

Even so, the needless deaths of so many young people is desperately sad. I found with Dom's death, and as Dr Carson wrote in 2016, for rappers, it's potentially a rich and fertile ground to write lamentable but creative lyrics on the people they cared about. I did find a song in the early style of rap that Dom listened to, written by Eminem, called *Difficult* (2006 – Appendix 8), about the death of the rapper's best friend. I wondered, with so many of them slain on the street, if drill rappers also wrote about their dead friends? How would it be different to my own ruminations, or even Eminem's? I searched Google and YouTube; I even watched a six-hour long YouTube video called (the)

BEST OF UK DRILL MUSIC 2016 @UkRapMashups. But I couldn't find anything remotely respectful about a lost friend. I saw angry, often masked, young men, just seeking attention and fame. After hours of listening to the relentless (same) beats and the incomprehensible words and rhymes, I would suggest that if they did write grief narratives, or even tried to put their case forward about poverty, they would have to leave the argot of drill. If the violence is because they are being marginalised and not about the music, if they want to be taken seriously by the mainstream or by their local and political leaders, if they want to encourage a wider and more culturally sympathetic audience to act, they will need to engage with society to try to convince them to change. Not kill each other.

In my reflections I'd missed the end of the London knife crime report and the broadcast was now a live feed from the Christmas market at Strasbourg. The news reporter was delivering some horrific news about a gunman on the run and potentially three dead at the market. I flicked the channel to another one, and the news anchor on that news feed was delivering a story from St Werburgh's City Farm. The reporter was explaining that a group of protesters, holding 'They wanted to Live' signs, had held a candle lit vigil handing out vegan mince pies to passers-by. 'Well,' I thought, 'perhaps the rappers with dead friends have made an impact after all?' The anchor continued; it seems the protestors were vegans and were there to mourn nine turkeys that had been killed ahead of Christmas, not the growing list of dead children on our streets. I switched the TV off, put our hunting knives back in their sheaths, and returned them back to the toolbox in the garage.

# William 'Eric' Hall (1938–2020), Newbiggin, 5 February

> …they only are heathen who, having great ideals, do not live up to them… Every soul is engaged in a Great Work – the labor of personal liberation from the state of ignorance. The world is a great prison and its bars are the Unknown. Each is a prisoner until, at last, he earns the right to tear these bars from their moldering sockets and pass, illuminated and inspired into the darkness, which becomes lighted by that presence. (Manly Palmer Hall)

I suspect Manly Palmer and Eric are not related. MP Hall was an author, lecturer, astrologer and mystic, born in Canada on 18 March 1901. William 'Eric' Hall was a Cumbrian lad, painter and decorator, armchair philosopher, and font of knowledge related to all things DIY. When do we see the light that MP Hall refers to? This is where the two Halls and Dominic connect. Sometimes that light is in someone we know or we meet for the first time.

Today is Eric's funeral. His mortal light was extinguished suddenly on 25 January. He collapsed on his garden pathway while walking from his car. I didn't know this at the time, but feared the worst when I saw a police car parked up over the road. Two policemen left his house at 10 pm. Eric was eighty-one and had been ill for eighteen months. As far as I know, his illness wasn't diagnosed even up to the doctor's visit on the day of his sudden death. Prior to this, Eric was a very knowledgeable, happy, energetic and busy man. He helped us out several times after we moved into Beech House.

This morning I'm at my desk writing and looking out of the window. The pallbearers carried Eric's coffin from one end of the village to the other, then placed it carefully into the waiting hearse outside his cottage opposite Beech House. His son, Peter, and son-in-law, Colin, were two of the four bearers.

They slowly drove to Carlisle. Six of Dom's pals carried his coffin from Penrith High Street, Middlegate, to St Andrew's Church, two hundred metres away. They were all twenty-two or twenty-three years of age, and took their responsibilities mega seriously, as Dom would say. Eric didn't make the journey from home to St Andrew's church. He was cremated at Carlisle, twenty miles away. The cortège made its way back to Penrith without him. Nevertheless, the close family and mourners walked the same two hundred meters to the church that we had with Dom. Even so, Eric's presence was felt in the vaulted room and the stories of his life, which dominated the next hour.

The service reminded me of Dom's funeral six years earlier. Not because it was held in the same church, not because Eric wasn't there – Dom's coffin was front and centre – but because he was there in spirit. The passion and love that Eric's son, daughter and grandchildren expressed for him compared to the homage at Dom's service. Reuben played his guitar and sang a song he'd written about his brother. Chloe, Linzi, Dom's friends and I all stood in front of the eagle lectern and remembered him. For Eric, Victoria and Rebecca wrote a poem about Grandad, 'L'arl Hally', as most of the room knew him, and Victoria read it to the mourners. Debra, his daughter, read the verses of *The Last Farewell*, a song written in 1971 by Ron Webster, and performed by Roger Whittaker, a British folk singer. It sold ten million copies, and it described Eric perfectly. One in a million. A shining light. I believe that Eric and Dom lived up to their ideals and became examples to us all. And lastly, Peter spent an hour speaking eloquently about his dad's life. There were some heart-warming and forgotten memories for many, and some hidden history for others. Marj, Peter's mother, didn't know that when Peter worked in the family business Eric sacked him, but only after Peter announced he was leaving the firm. Eric had to win.

The love shared between family and friends was overwhelming, again reminding me of Dom's funeral. Despite Eric being eighty-one, the church was almost as full as it was for Dom's service. That's the measure of the man. Six years and three months ago, I stood behind that same eagle lectern as Peter had and spoke about my son. My heart ached and I wished the roles could be reversed, that Dom could have stood there speaking eloquently about his dad instead. I know he would never have created our literary DNA. I wouldn't expect him to. He never wrote much, but he did text and post on social media phonetically and prolifically. I would definitely be added to his digital footprint; perhaps it would be our shared 'digital DNA'? Secretly though, I wondered, if Dom had been up there behind the eagle in 2013, my coffin in front of him, what he would have said about his dad? Would I have been 'L'arl Lofty'?

The morning of the day he was killed, Dom dropped me back home after we delivered his car to the garage. He had a stinking flu, high temperature and a consistent cough. I remember thinking selfishly that I hoped he didn't pass it on. He didn't; at least I can't remember having the flu after he died. I told him to take a few days off. He refused. He had an old age pensioner's boiler repair to do, and he didn't want to let her down. The pot-washer at the Sportsmans had gone back home to Poland for a holiday, so Dom had volunteered to cover his shift that night too.

We do everything we can to recall the memories of our loved one. As I wrote earlier, we even try to connect unrelated things to them. Today, in my head I try to associate Covid-19 and Dominic. It's another way, another reason to keep him in my thoughts, to talk to him and about him. This pandemic is changing the way we live and has brought the familiar world to a standstill. It's affecting every part of our lives. Shielding, self-isolating and social distancing have all been introduced to reduce human contact. Workers are losing their jobs, companies are closing their doors, schools and universities are stopping lectures. Exams are on hold. The elderly and infirm are the most vulnerable. The UK government has suggested that they stay at home to try to stay safe. But as I write this, it's the elderly and vulnerable who are dying.

From a Loftus family perspective, Susan was told last night to work from home until further notice, three months minimum. Reuben has decided to stay in London – he didn't want to infect his parents – even though the city will be locked down tonight. Forty underground stations will be closed until further notice. The Night Tube will stop running, and twenty-thousand troops are on standby. Chloe left Australia in November last year and has been slowly travelling back to the UK from Sydney via Asia. She arrived in India last week, and has been sending messages every day since, mainly wondering what to do about the pandemic and if she should return home.

My advice to both children has been to 'stay calm'.

Six years after Dom was killed, how do I connect him to Covid-19 in 2019? When he died, our world was brought to a standstill. It affected every part of our lives, and like Coronavirus, it changed the way we lived. Unlike grief, the virus will disappear, and society will re-engage at some point. But, like the aftermath of grief, society will be different, and we will return to a different normality. If I leave the shadow that is cast by Dom's death, will I stop re-living that day and will my life improve?

I look at the pictures around the house in a new light, especially the one where Dom is raising a glass to the photographer beside the 'Glendale'. As I look at it, it makes me smile for the first time. I suspect Dom would have been stoic about the virus. His dust mask and latex gloves would have been put on, old ladies would still have had their boilers serviced – as long as they made a cuppa and kept two metres away. He might not have been an essential front-line worker, but no appointments would have been cancelled, missed or rearranged, whether the UK government liked it or not. Not on Dom's watch.

# Denise

I wrote to Sir Lindsay Hoyle, the Speaker of the House of Commons, just after he'd taken over from John Bercow. I enclosed an essay I'd written about him and his daughter. She'd taken her own life three years earlier. It was a very personal piece so I wrote and asked his permission to include it in my memoir. It was the right thing to do. His assistant wrote back with a nice letter. The speaker was moved, but declined the offer, and said he'd rather not have the work included in the memoir.

After Dom's death, I too received lots of letters from other people who had lost someone close. They offered written support and a kind of 'after-life kindred spirit'. I liked what I'd written in the creative piece so I was disappointed Hoyle said no. I thought later that my letter to him was also a morbid kindred spirit reaching out, and perhaps that was a step too far. I accepted Sir Lindsay's wishes, so this space remained blank from 9 November 2019. I didn't consider occupying the vacant space again. It remained Hoyle-less until March 2020.

At that point I had bought and read *Time Lived, Without Its Flow* (2011) by Denise Riley. I have a revised and signed copy (2019) from Waterstones, so Denise must have made a visit recently to Carlisle, her hometown, and I'd missed her. I was also drawn to it because of the introduction by Max Porter. Denise, a critically acclaimed poet and philosopher, published the book four years after her adult son Jake died suddenly of an undiagnosed heart condition. Just like the opening lines from *A Grief Observed*, her words were equally as honest and also addressed her grief directly. Her book encouraged me to look at death in a different way; she said:

> I'll not be writing about death, but about an altered condition of life. The experience that not only preoccupied but occupied me was of living in suddenly arrested time: that acute sensation of being cut off from any temporal flow that can grip you after the sudden death of your child. And a child it seems, of any age. (p. 13)

Grief impacts our perceptions of time and space. It changes the language a grieving person uses. Time was also on my mind before I'd read Riley's book. I'd written about time and time travel, superimposing and imposing my own memories over Dom's life, trying to create, control and gift him new memories that he'll never have. Our thoughts cross here. Riley believes that she is living outside of time because for a parent, a child's time is 'quietly uncoiling inside your own' (p. 50), so when the child's life stops, 'the purely cognitive violence of it freezes the parent's time, too. She cannot 'move on' because 'there is no medium through which to move any more' (p. 41). She argues that coming close to your child's death is an existential risk to the survivor. I've been struggling over the last six years with who I am now, and who and what I will be in the future.

I contemplate Riley's book through the lens of after-life kindred spiritness while our paths and our interpretations of loss diverge for a moment. She hardly mentions Jake. I know he was an adult and he was at work when he died but not much more. On the other hand, I need to talk about Dom, bring him into my every conversation, even if the words are for my own consumption. I have to write poems and short stories about him. Riley does, however, capture our emotional condition. She manipulates our language and she sees our future alone much better than I do.

I do what I always do with Dom: I have a thought, hear a song, smell a smell, see a movie and I want to associate it with him. Even before Riley's diary begins, before she creates their literary DNA, I go back and find that line in her book that resonates with me, and we are one again:

> But how can such a striking condition ever be voiced? It runs wildly counter to everything that I'd thought we could safely assume about lived time. So, this 'arrested time' is also a question about what is describable; about the linguistic limits of what can be conveyed. (p. 14)

This, I fear, is the nub of the problem that grieving writers face. How can we do justice to our dead child, parent or lover, when we can't find the words? I dread this more now than the risk of being in danger of taking my own life. Doomed to be remembered as a poetaster, or worse still, Dom not to be remembered at all. Grief memoir is the meta narrative antidote of these emotions and fears; it is the all-encompassing theme that keeps our stories together. If as writers we can embrace it, perhaps we can find the right words or the language to keep our loved one's memory alive. If we can't, how can we expect non-writers to express their grief in everyday terms. As my memoir is a creative–critical piece of work, the reader might find some words within it that will resonate and help them express their own loss.

# Grief, Melancholia and Theories – the Search for Meaning

In his paper *Grief as a Psychiatric Disorder* (2012), Richard A Bryant discusses the need for a careful diagnosis of grief. On one hand, grief can be seen as a ubiquitous human behaviour, or 'normal', as Nowinski (2012) suggests. On the other Neimeyer et al. argue from a constructivist perspective, a postmodern approach to psychology, that suggests grief is a social construct and our religious beliefs or culture affect how we mourn (2004). Neimeyer further states that the context of a loss, such as sudden, violent or meaningless death, like the death of a child, also affects how the bereaved tries to reconstruct their self-narrative. I would suggest also that there are further circumstances that will have an impact on the depth or level of grief. For example, are we more successful at coming to terms with the death of an ageing aunt who has ailed for years and dies quietly in bed, than the sudden unexpected death of a twenty-two-year-old son?

The main emphasis of constructivism is that people need to impose meaning on their life experiences (Neimeyer, 2009). A fundamental proposition of constructivism is that humans are motivated to construct and maintain a meaningful self-narrative. An individual's identity is therefore essentially a narrative achievement, as our sense of self is established through the stories that we construct about ourselves and share with others. Through this, Viktor Frankl (1992) argues, we pursue a quest for meaning as the key to our mental health and human flourishing (p. 157).

Frankl, a holocaust survivor, certainly understood the search for meaning. In his 1946 book, *Man's Search for Meaning*, he chronicles his time in a Nazi concentration camp and tells his story about finding spiritual survival. Humans are natural storytellers, more so when constructing their own self-narrative, which is a kind of internal storyboard of how we live and view our lives. When someone is removed from our narrative arc, we have to rewrite or reimagine our story with a different ending. There are two meaning making strategies within constructivism that enable this reinvention process; the first is 'narrative retelling', which offers a way through which the bereaved can integrate the loss into the story of their lives in a meaningful way, at the same time keeping a degree of rationality in their experience during their mourning period and beyond. This process is normally managed by a professionally trained therapist in a safe environment. The second approach is 'therapeutic writing', the main focus of this chapter.

However, meaning making can be traced back to Socrates original ideas of the importance of knowing yourself, questioning your beliefs and living your life with high moral standards. His ideas were built on by the philosopher Zeno of Citium around 300 BC, and then further developed in the first century by the Roman philosophers Seneca and Epictetus. Central to Stoicism, is the acknowledgment that most of what happens to us is out of our control, and what we can control is how we view what happens to us. Epictetus said 'Men are disturbed not by things but by their opinions about them.' Frankl, therefore argues that we cannot avoid suffering but we can choose how to cope with it, find meaning in it and move forward with renewed purpose. At the heart of his theory is logotherapy, which is a form of existential analysis that proposes that the primary human drive is not pleasure but the pursuit of what we find meaningful.

For the subset of individuals who do search for meaning, it appears that meaning does not come easily. One study of parents whose children have suffered sudden infant death found that only 23% who searched for meaning in the early months of bereavement claimed to have found any in the years that followed, and in subsequent interviews many reported ceasing their unproductive search altogether (McIntosh et al., 1993). When the bereaved are successful in finding meaning, evidence indicates that they fare better than those who struggle to make sense of the experience. Studies have reported that finding meaning is related to less intense grief (Schwartzberg and Janoff-Bulman, 1991), higher subjective well-being (Stein et al., 1997) and more positive immune system functioning (Bower et al., 2003). In their study of bereaved parents, Murphy et al. (2003) showed that finding meaning was related to lower mental distress, higher marital satisfaction and better physical health. Overall, research has demonstrated that many individuals engage in a quest for meaning following a bereavement, and suggests that bereaved people struggling to make sense of their loss could benefit from interventions that nurture this process.

Psychologists and clinicians have often linked traumatic experiences with subsequent physical and mental health problems. The more extreme the trauma and the length of time over which it lasts are predictors of Post-Traumatic Stress Disorder (PTSD) (Breslau, Chilcoat, Kessler and Davis, 1999). It is also generally agreed that people prone to PTSD also have had a history of depression, trauma and other PTSD episodes in the past, even prior to their most recent traumatic experience (Miller, 2003). On the first page of my memoir, even before I started any research on grief, I felt that my grief was what I imagined Post-Traumatic Stress Disorder would feel like. In western culture, one of the biggest distresses we can experience in life is the death of someone close, particularly an unexpected or early death. If anything was going to trigger PTSD in me, I decided it would be that.

John James (1944–2021), who founded the Grief Institute in the mid-eighties and is the author of the *Grief Recovery Method* (eBook, no date), argues that grief is not a clinical depression. His eBook is a list of sixty-one 'tips' on the experience of grief and how to help people through it. John lost his son in 1977 and struggled to find grief support, ultimately coming up with his own recovery method to deal with his loss. In point thirteen of the guide, he notes that 'grief is normal and natural, it is not a pathological condition or a personality disorder'. He also states in point fourteen that 'Grief is often mislabelled as ADHD, Depression, PTSD, and many other pathological conditions.' Whilst I agree that grief is normal, and that everyone will grieve at some point in their lives, and it's not a pathological condition, there is nevertheless disagreement within medicine that PTSD is pathological. It's often confused with substance use disorder (SUD), which in my own experience follows after and because of the grief, not before.

Pathology is the study of disease, such as cancer, cardiovascular disease, congenital, hereditary, neonatal diseases and abnormalities, even animal disease. Grief is none of those.

John's point that 'grief is often mislabelled' is interesting: there are even clinical misconceptions about grief. Whilst *Grief Recovery Method* is not dated, from other dates on his website, his book was written between thirty and forty years ago, so today I think there would be fewer misdiagnoses than he claims. A GP who diagnoses a fifty-six-year-old grieving father with ADHD, which is one of the most common neurodevelopmental disorders of childhood, is not asking the right questions, or getting the right answers. Whilst ADHD can last into adulthood, it's usually first diagnosed in childhood. Even diagnosing a child who had recently lost a parent and who had no previous ADHD symptoms with ADHD would be a difficult decision to make. Whilst ADHD and grief may have similar symptoms, for example, trouble concentrating or paying attention, that's where it ends.

Despite lacking any formal psychological or medical training, John James is internationally recognised as one of the foremost authorities on grief and grief recovery. He has co-authored multiple publications on the topic of recovery from loss: *The Grief Recovery Handbook* (no date), *When Children Grieve* (1997), *Moving On, Moving Beyond Loss* (2010), and *The Grief Recovery Handbook for Pet Loss* (2014). Despite his non-clinical background, he was well respected in grief work, so if the *Grief Recovery Method* has helped him and others through their grief, that's perfectly laudable.

On the other hand, John James's eBook was written as a complete guide for people who are grieving to try to help them deal with their grief; on this he makes some clinical assertions and assumptions. With regard to these, I would argue that grief is more complex than John states. There are a number of internal factors that influence how we experience and deal with grief including psychological, spiritual, physical, interpersonal and behavioural ones. These factors can have an impact on health and wellbeing. Psychologically, personal upheavals provoke intense and long-lasting emotional changes. Unexpected events are generally associated with cognitive disruption including ruminating as an attempt to understand what happened and why. Traumas can cause disruptions to people's social networks. Due in part to these social and psychological changes, traumas also cause negative lifestyle changes such as excessive smoking, drinking and substance abuse. There is also a potential disruption to sleeping and eating patterns (Pennebaker, J. W. and Chung, C. K., 2005).

Pennebaker's extensive research and publications are centred on treating trauma in general, and not specifically grief as a traumatic experience. He does nevertheless focus on the positive effects of therapeutic writing to aid trauma and other posttraumatic stresses, which include anxiety, depression, obsessive-compulsive disorder, alcohol and substance abuse, eating disorders, interpersonal relationship issues and low self-esteem (Farooqui, 2016).

It wasn't until the 1980s, after the James Pennebaker's 'expressive writing' trials, that writing-as-therapy was considered a serious method of clinical practice (US). Even prior to the trials there was overwhelming evidence going as far back as Freud's paper *Creative Writers and Day-Dreaming* (1907). Freud argued that keeping a journal or writing creatively, whilst not a 'cure' for grief, did facilitate healing. Despite this, in the UK, although music therapy, dance movement therapy, drama therapy and visual art therapy all have recognised professional bodies which provide regulation and codes of practice for members, therapeutic writing still remains unregulated and without a statutory code of practice. Whilst accredited courses are emerging, poetry therapy, for example, is still not a recognised profession in the UK.

The US journal Psychology Today has been a core text for me over the last seven years. It contains a great deal of the research and current thinking about grief. It also chronicled the conflicting theories about grief over the last forty years. In her paper *Grief Can Last a Lifetime. Is grief an illness?* (2012), Phyllis R Silverman argues that grief isn't an illness, including Prolonged Grief Disorder (PGD). In her book she agrees with Freud, writing that there is no treatment that can lead to a 'cure'.

I agree with Freud and Silverman, there isn't a cure for grief, it's something that as other sufferers of PGD and the father of a dead son, I'll never actually fully recover from. However, I think it's disingenuous of

Silverman to say that because there is no cure, grief is not an illness. Would she then also suggest this about conditions such as heart disease, stroke, and respiratory infections which are survivable, but account for the majority of deaths each year around the world? In some respects, prolonged grief is just as frightening and draining on your life as being told that you have cancer.

Nevertheless, Silverman's view is supported by others including Joseph Nowinski. In his paper 'Should Grief Be a Mental Illness'? Where to draw the line between grief and mental illness? (2012), Nowinski argues:

> We should continue our cultural tradition of recognising grief as a normal (and expected) human experience. It may also vary in intensity and duration from person to person, depending on the nature of the loss. If anything, the grieving person may benefit from support and sympathy, rather than being diagnosed as pathological and treated as such. (par. 9)

However, Nowinski starts his paper with a rhetorical question, asking his fellow psychologists how they would diagnose a patient who says, 'I haven't been sleeping well. I don't have much of an appetite and I've lost a few pounds in the last month. I feel sad most of the time and once a day I find myself crying. Basically, it's all I can do every morning to get myself out of bed and start the day' (Nowinski, 2012). Those words echo an early conversation I had with Colin, my bereavement counsellor. They are also classic symptoms of clinical depression.

James Kaufman, associate professor of California State University (2001), conducted a retrospective study of 1,629 writers, which showed that poets, specifically female poets, were more likely than non-fiction writers, playwrights and fiction writers to have some type of mental illness. This link between creativity and mental illness is now frequently referred to as 'The Sylvia Plath Effect' (Kaufman, 2001). In contrast, Professor Albert Rothenberg agrees there are indeed many creative people who suffer from mental illness, but says, 'although comprised of an impressive membership, the list is dwarfed by the very large number of highly creative people both in modern times and throughout history without evidence of a disorder, for example, Czeslaw Milosz, Henry Moore, Sigrid Undset, Jane Austen, Anton Chekhov, George Eliot, John Milton, and Johann Sebastian Bach'.

Rothenberg concedes that the solution to the conundrum of mental illness in creative individuals appropriately lies in the nature of the creative processes themselves. 'If the factors directly producing creations were in some way derived from, or even facilitated, by illness, there would then be a necessary connection.' (*Creativity and mental illness*. Am J Psychiatry, 1995)

Rothenberg (2002) also argues that 'it's only when the mind is clear from depression again that we are creative', i.e., when the brain is back to 'normal'. I would suggest that there is limited research on what would be termed the basic process of normal creativity. Furthermore, people who are able to think creatively demonstrate many of the traits associated with mental illness through the normal cognitive functions that people engage in when coming up with creative ideas. It's true that creative people can think outside the box, often have diverse associations and are uninhibited in their generation of ideas; Papworth, (2016) suggests they are able to selectively turn on and off the same thinking patterns that consistently plague people with persistent psychopathologies. However, the range of psychopathologies is vast, including eating disorders to gender dysphoria, to narcissism, so how can we reach a firm conclusion on which creatives are influenced by a particular behavioural disorder? For example, what was it that drove Hemmingway to sharpen 20 pencils every morning before he started writing? As a grieving creative writer, am I offered 'divine providence' to tell Dom's story, or is it as Plato, Socrates and Aristotle questioned, 'divine madness' of inspiration?

# Tick Tock

As I moved through my own grief, not knowing whether my writing was inspired by a godly intervention or godly inspiration, I examined twentieth and twenty-first century narratives and theories in order to understand if, and why grief, depression and self-expression are connected. Through my own ruminations and experiences, I came to believe that there are links between grief, depression and the benefits that self-expressive writing can bring to both. Why is this important? Suicide rates have increased by over 60% worldwide in the last 45 years, and the number of antidepressant prescriptions issued in the UK alone has risen to 64.7 million in 2016, more than double the number issued in 2006. It comes as no surprise that on the back of these escalating numbers, creative writing workshops for 'wellbeing', 'healing' or 'mindfulness' have increased all over the world.

 Reflecting on this increase of prescribing drugs to deal with depression, it seems normal for a GP to take this action. Shortly after Dom's death, I was prescribed antidepressants. I wasn't comfortable. They may have reduced my anxiety but they were suppressants that also drained me of any other emotion. Consequently, I didn't write much. Time seemed to be put on hold and I never felt the need to look at a clock. Despite becoming insentient, I continued to read, to try to educate myself. As well as psychology and clinical papers, I read narrative non-fiction, mainly grief memoirs such as the ones I've mentioned earlier. I found common threads, idioms and themes throughout the novels, with similar questions that their authors asked themselves. It's hard to know if any of the writers I've discussed throughout these pages reacted as I did and took to alcohol, or prescription or non-prescription drugs. If they did, it wasn't revealed in their narratives. I don't think they were being dishonest with the reader; it just wasn't as important as the writing. Nevertheless, three months in, I stopped taking the antidepressants and I too refocused on my writing.

 As I re-engaged, I noticed the clock again and its tick seemed louder. I was also able to narrow down some of the main tropes of grief memoir. By far the most repeated was the concept of time, and I also reflected on it in my own work. For some writers time stopped; for others it didn't matter anymore, or it just ceased to exist after a loved one's death. It froze; it had no further meaning. Memories became just as important as the future, and physical things like possessions or money had 'no value'. MacDonald wrote in H is for Hawk, 'Time didn't run forwards anymore. It was a solid thing you could press yourself against it and feel it push back; a thick fluid, half-air, half-glass, that flowed both ways and sent ripples of recollection forwards and new events backwards so that new things I encountered, then, seemed souvenirs from the distant past' (2014, p. 16).

My memoir doesn't have a traditional beginning, a middle or an end. In some respects, I ignore time because it's irrelevant, but as I mentioned, creative and self-expressive writing can be a non-invasive therapy to that loop of grief. Grief isn't linear and even today I still don't know whether my grief itself will have a conclusion. The memoir does however allow me to record the transitions in my life as I try to learn to cope without Dom in it. It chronicles the changes to my outlook on death and grief after Dom's death.

A part of that transformation was facilitated after I read a book from a strange source. It wasn't on my radar and not in the canon of grief, but I came to it by reading Tragedy of the Little Darlings, an essay by Douglas Murray. He'd written about JM Barrie and the life and death of a real boy called Peter that inspired him to write Peter Pan. Murry also wrote the introduction of a book I'd bought but not read. I'd picked it up at the book shop because it was published by Notting Hill Editions, which is a publishing house based in Kendal, near where I live.

The book, *Confessions of a Heretic* (2016) by Sir Roger Scruton (1944–2020), is a collection of random, unconnected but provocative essays. Two of the essays stood out.

The first, *Dying in Time*, is a profound meditation on death. I was drawn to it by the word 'time'. Scruton writes, 'the main point, it seems to me, is to maintain an active life of risk and affection remembering always that the value of life does not consist in its length but in its depth' (p. 141). So, Scruton seems to suggest that time is not important, and since 2013, I've focused on the length of Dom's life and not the breadth of his story. I've told stories about him; I've even written a few film scripts (story lines and treatments, really) that Dom features in. In the early stories he played a cameo role, then later he became the main protagonist. But because I'd started writing this non-fiction about Dom's life, these scripts are gathering virtual dust on iCloud. Script writing was something I wanted to pick up again after I'd finished Dom's story, so I kept an eye on various blogs and websites including BBC Maestro (www.bbcmaestro.com).

One of the maestros is Jed Mercurio (OBE), a titan of British TV broadcasting and a writer. I'd joined one of his short courses called 'Writing Drama for TV'. Early on in the video he confesses he's more scientist than artist. He'd studied medicine at Birmingham. During the module 'Character and Settings', he explained how useful his scientific training has been in this planning stage. He describes how characters, especially big or important ones, have impact on the setting, and he does this by taking his audience through Einstein's *Theory of Relativity* (1915). He defines the effects of space and time and shows how they can be changed depending how the character moves within that space.

Before Einstein's theory, people thought space was a stage on which things happened. We could throw in some stars or planets like actors, and they would move around on this stage. I liked Mercuria's connection to drama and storytelling, but Einstein realised that space wasn't as passive as that. It's dynamic and it responds to what's happening within it. If you put something heavy, such as Earth, in space, then the space around it gives a little. The presence of earth causes a small dent in space and in time as well. When something else moves close to Earth, such as the moon, it senses the dent and rolls around the earth like a golf ball rolling in an empty fruit bowl. This is gravity. As writers of grief, it is perhaps through this metaphor that we can explain how difficult it is to occupy the distance between us and the deceased. They inhabit a space in our lives whilst they are living, but as Einstein suggests, space and time are inextricably linked, so when we lose a loved one, the dent they leave in our lives will always be unbreachable.

Scruton's *Dying in Time* is actually a consideration of his own death. He's contemplating when is a timely moment for someone to die, specifically when is the right time for him to die. Before that, he suggests a contraposition to society's quest for 'eternal life' by reminding us that Nietzsche formulated the idea of a timely death as a fundamental part of his morality, and that longevity might erode what we value in life, the achievements and the affections that give us purpose. Scruton writes, 'A life is an object of judgement, like a work of art; and judgement means viewing it from outside, as the life of another' (p. 127). He suggests that rather than being a burden on family and society, we should 'go out' on a high. This is his moral point of view, and it reverberates with the words of Plato, Socrates et al., who tell us that we should 'Judge no man happy until he is dead'.

In life, we recognise individuals for achievements throughout their life, but in general we view life as a continuous drama, with a meaning that is defined by the whole of that life. This is what Plato, Socrates and Aristotle were referring to. They posited that the value of an individual life is a property of the whole life, and that death and dying are as much a part of it as the experiences that go before them. But what do they mean by happiness? They mean what you might expect them to mean. They are also suggesting that happiness can be reversed quite easily during our lives, for example by shame or humiliation. That view is decided by someone else but motivated by our actions. Scruton writes, 'Just as 'having a life' is a moral idea, so is 'losing a life.'' The secret of happiness is to die before that loss occurs. This has been demonstrated through history by the ancient Greeks, the Japanese, as recently as the Second World War, the Romans and the Anglo-Saxons. All their societies believed that death was preferable to a shameful survival.

I can't help thinking about my heroes and the people I have admired, and strangely they are people who have been taken early and without experiencing public shame or humiliation, or, if there was anything suspicious in their past, it has been airbrushed out by their death. People like James Dean, Jimi Hendrix, JFK and Amy Winehouse. They are all high achievers, but their places in history have been cemented by their deaths. Scruton takes his inspiration from Aristotle and the ancients, and from them he decides what disposition he needs to deal with the contingencies of life. These virtues cluster around a central core of prudence, courage, justice and temperance, which he suggests 'creates a moral robustness to our acceptability' in the eyes of others (p. 138). It's these people, after all, who decide if the life we have led has been a successful one.

I admire the depth of Scruton's thinking and work. Of all the things I've read in trying to understand my reaction to Dom's death, it's these two essays that have helped me draw some conclusions. Indeed, it's the philosophers in general, and not the grief counsellors or theorists that have allowed me to consider my position on Dom's death, or at least, to reconcile myself to his loss. Scruton assures us that 'life only becomes worthwhile through our relations with others, in which mutual affection and esteem lift our actions from the realm of appetite, and endow them with significance'. This is the reason we gloss over the whispered bad boy/girl images of James Dean, Jimi Hendrix, JFK and Amy Winehouse, as they move from flawed mortals to immortality. How then do I assure Dominic's immortality?

Until Dom died, I too thought I was immortal, but only because I had never thought about my own death. It's only now I realise that I should have considered what death is and what it means. Long before clinical or psychological intervention, it has been the role of the philosopher to show us how we should think of death so we can overcome our fear of it. Epicurus (341–270 BC) argues that there is nothing to fear in death, as death is nothing: 'I do not survive it, so there is nothing bad for me on the other side of it. In an important sense death doesn't happen to me: when I am, death is not; and when death is, I am not'. At the point of writing this essay, Scruton was seventy-two, as opposed to Dom's twenty-two, so has had much longer to reflect on how he should face his death. Dom had no choice in his.

Scruton's second essay, 'Mourning Our Losses: Reflections on Strauss's Metamorphosen', concludes by saying, '[Metamorphosen]…is a work without hope, and without any promise for the future. Yet for all that it is a great work of art, and one that still speaks to us' (p. 122). The essay is an insightful read.

Many of Scruton's assertions and observations are laser sharp. He draws comparisons with Richard Strauss's work, amongst other pieces, which is a reason why he finishes the essay on that mixed note. The essay begins with a discussion of Freud's essay 'Mourning and Melancholia' (1918). Freud argues that until the work of mourning is accomplished, it's impossible to engage in a new life, new loves and a new engagement with the world. After conducting my research in this area, I find that this message underpins all the grief theories written since Freud. Scruton admits that he doesn't fully support Freud's views, but on this occasion, he does, and he gives examples of losing a parent or child and the existential losses that can bring.

Freud believes that mourning is an act of redemption, and as I've come to realise in writing about Dom, all elegies – whether we read them out at the church or write them as part of a literary recovery process – are designed to highlight virtues and minimise faults or vices. Scruton notes that mourning is also an act of reconciliation and forgiveness in which the dead person is given retrospective permission to die. But what if the dead person can't be forgiven? Does mourning becomes impossible? Metamorphosen was written just before the end of the Second World War, and Scruton drew comparisons with the collective mourning of the German people after the war and the meaning behind Strauss's study for twenty-three solo strings.

Scruton suggests that after the war, the immovable memory of Hitler's Germany and its crimes against humanity wouldn't allow the Germans to grieve for their dead, and at the same time, accept the guilt that the dead had gathered to themselves. The accepted story about Strauss's piece is that he composed it following the bombing and destruction of Germany, in particular the Munich Hoftheatre. While the rest of the country was struggling to mourn, Strauss's work invited a more general mourning of sorts.

On page 121 of his essay Scruton writes about elegy: '…this we were given, and it is gone, but we should be grateful for it, and try to live up to its memory'. This gave me hope about my own mourning, but page 117 gave me a further insight into letting go. Scruton draws a comparison with Metamorphosen and Thomas Mann's Doctor Faustus (1947). As a contemporary of Strauss, Mann's book also is a response to the destruction of

Germany. Doctor Faustus is the story of Adrian Leverkuhn, a musician who sells his soul to the devil. It's a reworking of Faust, a fragment (Goethe, 1790) and, as is the case with Faustian tales, Leverkuhn gives up some long-term benefits for short-term gain. He agrees to twenty-four years of musical fame, but in return, he loses something that is ultimately more valuable than what he has gained. He relinquishes his ability to love his fellow man. However, the message of Dr Faustus, for me at least, is one of hope. Scruton explains it thus: 'we can lose everything; but if we are still conscious of that loss and what it means, then there is something that we have not lost. All is not lost if art remains, to show that all is not lost' (p. 117).

Throughout his life, Scruton had reservations about religion and Christianity (*Gentle Regrets: Thoughts from a Life,* 2005). As a lay theologian, it's also one of the things CS Lewis struggles with in *A Grief Observed*. He questioned but never doubted his belief in God; however, grief caused an existential crisis and it challenged everything he'd written and believed in. This is how I felt after Dom died. Everything I knew or believed was turned on its head. I didn't understand or see the usefulness in anything anymore.

Religiosity can take many forms. I found faith and comfort in the Cumbrian landscape as Lewis did in Herefordshire. The Lake District is an environment that has physically remained untouched for tens of thousands of years. There are fields of drumlins that surround Vicargate, where Dom grew up. He knew these hill-lets formed by glaciers thousands of years ago like the back of his hand, and it's in the knowledge of that where I found some solace and consolation. From a small child he was able to see and enjoy the mountains and lakes every day. As I drove around Cumbria, or looked out the living room window, I actually began to resent the views: the shapes of the fells, the glacial valleys, the becks and the rivers beside which, he spent all his life. They're all still there as he left them, but he's not here to enjoy them.

In 1803, Robert Southey travelled to the Lakes to visit his brother-in-law and college friend Samuel Taylor Coleridge. Coleridge was an opium addict, and Southey's sister Sara was struggling to cope. Nonetheless, Southey was in awe of Coleridge and Wordsworth and stunned by the beauty of the countryside. He decided to stay. Southey and his family moved into Greta Hall in Keswick with Coleridge and his family. He came to see the Lake District as the 'symbol of the nation's covenant with God, thanking Him that he was born an Englishman'. If there was a God, I found myself agreeing he would be found in the Lakes. So, I started to seek writers and poets who also may have found comfort in the wilderness, or even found themselves in the wilderness, as Lewis did after his wife's death.

# Landscapes

The memoir *H is for Hawk* (2014) is not only about the landscape and countryside of the Brecklands, north-east of Cambridge; the author finds herself in a personal wilderness after a loss. Before becoming a best-selling author in 2014, Helen Macdonald was a historian with a deep interest in English landscapes, especially the countryside, the wilderness and the history of falconry. In H is for Hawk (2014), she observes the ways that these things change continuously over time, and as in Denise Riley's *Time Lived, Without Its Flow* (2012), time is a theme that runs throughout. The book is about the death of Macdonald's father and fellow hawk trainer. Like *Levels of Life,* it is part historical and part biographical, and like many people who grieve, Helen grapples with the grieving process through a diary which is predominately about the hard-won trust between a hawk and a human. Yet, she splices into her grief narrative a biographical account of her literary hero, fellow austringer and author of *The Sword in the Stone* (1938) TH White.

Macdonald and White both experience exhilaration and doubt in raising their goshawks; both fear rejection and loss and want desperately to escape the pain inherent in the human world. Her narrative jumps between the 1930s and the present day, utilising the passage of time to thematically link White's experiences to hers. Her story runs parallel to White's by collapsing time through their shared experiences, fears and desires, as opposed to Riley's essay, which describes how Riley is cut off from any temporal flow after the sudden death of her child.

During his time at Stowe school, White 'dropped out of the curious adult heterosexual competition' (p. 32), and Macdonald discusses the long hours of psychoanalysis White went through with a counsellor who had written to him telling him he could help. Certain that 'Bennet would cure him of all of it: his homosexuality, his unhappiness, his sense of feeling unreal, his sadism, all of it: all his confusions and fears', White almost falls in love with a barmaid. In their sessions, Bennet would take White back in time. It was a way of 'fixing things: uncovering past traumas, revisiting them and defusing their power' (p. 76).

We are told as grieving parents that 'time will heal'. It will only heal if we can go back in time as White did. We could stop our boy getting in that car, tell our wife to have the check-up four years earlier than she did, or warn our best friend not to go to the nightclub that night because there might be someone waiting for them there with a gun. White remained a homosexual and Dominic still got in the car. Unlike Riley, for whom time remained cut off, Macdonald tells us about her father, 'the quiet man in a suit with a camera on his shoulder', who stopped time 'by making pictures of the moving things of the world'.

Dom was also a quiet man. He had his earphones plugged in to his MP3 player and listened to music at every opportunity. He seemed to know the words to every song. A few songs on his player are old-style country music but mostly it is rap music. Many of the songs are written and performed by Eminem (AKA Slim Shady), a white rapper. I mentioned earlier a specific song called 'Difficult' that Dom often played. It was written by Eminem on the death of his best friend Proof, and it was his way of remembering him. Rap music isn't a genre I listen to, but I connected with the lyrics and Eminem's story in a few ways. Firstly, the artist and his music reminded me of Dom. Like Dom, he wasn't a good student. He was often in trouble and switched schools a few times as he spent his early childhood between parents, which made it difficult to make friends. Whilst Dom had lots of friends and an idyllic upbringing in the Cumbrian countryside, it's this struggle in a school environment that links them together for me. It's a familiar scenario with troubled talent, which is why it makes Eminem so attractive to many young kids like Dom. His first album 'Infinite' sold less than a thousand copies. His second album was the first rap album ever to be nominated 'Album of the Year', selling more than 8 million copies in the United States alone.

    Secondly, there are many similarities between Eminem's sentiments and meaning-making in his lyrics and my thoughts and writing after Dom was killed. When someone is taken suddenly, as both Dom and Proof were, for both Eminem and me there was the immediate regret that we didn't tell them that we loved them as often as we should, and Eminem is very clear on that: 'I never got to say I love you as much as I wanted to, but I do' (line 6). Sudden, unexpected death shatters our worldview and eventually initiates this meaning-making in an attempt to make sense of our new life and roles (Park, 2010). It's tough to tell another man you love them, even if it's your son. Eminem knows that Proof isn't there to hear the song, so perhaps that makes it easier for him to write it.

Eminem and I come from a working-class background, with divorced parents. We are from different age groups and different cultures. Nevertheless, the words and his outpouring of grief resonated with me. Most of the lyrics are memories of their growing up together. I associate this with Walter's theory in *New Models of Grief* (1996). It is Eminem's lasting memorial to Proof.

In grief, we associate or experience 'associated behaviour' (Strobe and Shut, 1999). For example, when we visit places: in verse three Eminem writes about '54', which is a studio in Detroit where Eminem used to record. As Eminem does in the last lines of verse three, we listen to music that triggers sorrow. The association for me is I know that Dominic would have played this song many times, and I want to listen to something he has listened to. I want to feel closer to him. The dual-process model (Strobe and Shut, 1999) focuses on grieving processes and acknowledges the uniqueness of each individual and the way in which culture and gender may affect how a person grieves. In line five, all Eminem can do is look at pictures of Proof, as Susan did at the beginning with Dom. I was different; I had to force myself to look away as I couldn't look into Dom's eyes.

Before Eminem and their friend Obie went to Proof's funeral, they stood in the car park of the club where he was shot. They fired a pistol into the air and drank some alcohol in his memory. |In verse three line twenty-three, they 'Pour some liquor out' as an act of reverence. As a cultural response to a death, this ritual can be traced back to ancient Egypt. There, they often used water instead of alcohol. Water was symbolic as a life-giving liquid. With Eminem and his friends, their general practice was to pour out a little of whatever liquid they were consuming, then drink the rest. We know much about the ancient Egyptian tradition because of the Papyrus of Ani, a scroll dating back to around 1250 BC. It contains the following passage:

> Pour libation for your father and mother who rest in the valley of the dead. Do not forget to do this even when you are away from home. For as you do for your parents, your children will do for you.

Reading that takes me back to Dom's graveside. I don't necessarily agree with it, but there has been a very stylish matt finished silver bottle of Jägermeister hidden amongst the ever-changing cut flowers from day one. I just know that his friends will have gathered there and they will have performed the same ritual at the first opportunity, without the firearm.

Finally, I don't know if Eminem has read CS Lewis's *A Grief Observed*, but one thing they have in common is that they both question the decision made by God to take their loved ones. Lewis's faith is shaken but deep down he knows that his wife's death is a test and a trial. He wrote:

> 'Not that I am (I think) in much danger of ceasing to believe in God. The real danger is of coming to believe such dreadful things about Him. The conclusion I dread is not 'So there's no God after all,' but 'So this is what God's really like. Deceive yourself no longer.' (p. 2)

I wish I'd talked to Dom about the music he listened to, and although 'Difficult' and 'Message' are both full of foul language, spelling mistakes, colloquialisms and clichés, they both demonstrate the depth of Eminem's feelings and Dom would have been well aware of that. The lyrics are simple but the depth comes from their integrity and like 'My Friend', the anonymous poem left at Dom's graveside, the simplicity adds to the work's effect.

Rap music and the ghettos of Detroit are a far cry from the English Lakes or the world of CS Lewis. Nevertheless, grief, grief culture and our response to it can be the same. Royce Da, Eminem and Proof's friend, is quite open, as I have been in my memoir, and he says that life without his friend isn't worth living and sometimes it's difficult to carry on without him. This was a response from several of the other writers reviewed in my analysis, but I was surprised to find it in rap music. Many of these young men have known violence all their lives, whether at home or on the streets, yet for them, Lewis, Barnes, Didion, MacDonald and for me, grief, it seems, doesn't discriminate.

An important theme that came through particularly with CS Lewis and Julian Barnes, and touched on by Royce Da, was suicide. It was avoided by many, but Barnes wrote:

> The question of suicide arrives early, and quite logically. Most days I pass the stretch of pavement I was looking across at when the idea first came to me. I will give it x months, or x years (up to a maximum of two), and then, if I cannot live without her, if my life is reduced to mere passive continuance, I shall become active. (p. 79)

In the first year or so following Dom's death, my own thoughts were similar to Barnes, as I constantly assessed how and why I should continue to live. We differ in as far as Barnes was suffering because he'd lost his wife, the woman he loved for twenty-nine years. They'd experienced most things together and their lives were entwined and inseparable as lovers. I suffered because Dom had only lived for twenty-two years and I lamented everything in life he'd not been able to experience.

In *The Year of Magical Thinking* Didion also discusses suicide. She doesn't reveal her own thoughts about taking her own life, but writes about the fragility of life, quoting the phrase 'the apparent inadequacy of the precipitating event'. She is referring to Karl Menninger and what he wrote on suicide in *Man Against Himself* (1956). Menninger described the tendency among suicides to overreact to what might seem ordinary, even predictable circumstances. He cites a young woman who becomes depressed and kills herself after cutting her hair. He mentions a man who kills himself because he has been advised to stop playing golf, a child who commits suicide because his canary died and a woman who kills herself after missing two trains. 'In these instances,' Menninger writes, 'the hair, the golf, and the canary had an exaggerated value, so that when they were lost or when there was even a threat that they might be lost, the recoil of severed emotional bonds was fatal' (p. 232).

Didion and MacDonald also felt 'lost', that life wasn't worth going on with. In her memoir Didion wrote:

Geese had been observed reacting to such a death by flying and calling, searching until they themselves became disoriented and lost. Human beings, I read but did not need to learn, showed similar patterns of response. They searched. They stopped eating. They forgot to breathe. They grew faint from lowered oxygen; they clogged their sinuses with unshed tears and ended up in otolaryngologists' offices with obscure ear infections. They lost concentration. (p. 45)

It wasn't until I was re-reading a section of Dr Worden's book on grief, that I realised Didion was referring to work started by Charles Darwin's research in the nineteenth century and his book *The Expression of Emotions in Man and Animals* (1872). He described how sorrow is expressed by animals as well as humans. It was the ethologist Konrad Lorenz (1963) who actually described the grief behaviour in the separation of a greylag goose from its mate. Both Lorenz and Didion concluded that the goose's behaviour was roughly identical to her (human) behaviour in the same situation.

Until Dom's death, my experience of grief was limited. Losing a grandma in 1976 and my estranged biological father in 2003, I was sad, but Dom's death was a tsunami. It flattened my life. Like most people going through bereavement, there is very little guidance and I was swept along by the pain without a buoyancy aid. Ironically, I was kept alive by the thoughts of how I might end it all. Without knowing it, I was following John James's path after his infant son died, and was researching and writing my own Grief Recovery Method.

Dominic was killed on 3 October 2013. I didn't know then, but I can conclude now in 2023, that writing has enabled me to survive his death. We have photos of him all round the house. There are VHS and digital videos of him, filmed at every stage and every important event throughout his life.

Nevertheless, I was still compelled to write down as much as I could about our relationship before he died and at the same time, record my ongoing relationship with him after his death. I didn't want to forget. Over the last seven years, as well as writing, I've researched grief and the process of learning to live with it, as a way to try to make sense of the extraordinary, sometimes overwhelming feelings, emotions and fear that swamped me. I tried to put into perspective a world which had turned on its head. A child is not meant to die before a parent.

As discussed earlier, there has been a long-established link between mental illness and creativity. As Simonton points out in *Ruminations about mental illness and creativity* (2016), 'the looser a domain's constraints are for defining what is creative, the more we tend to find instances of people with various psychoses operating 'creatively' within that domain'. Secondly, as Kinney and Richards, Schlesinger, Carson and Abraham discuss (2016), there seems to be a shared vulnerability or a 'third variable' that is associated with the thinking styles of the mentally ill and what led to their creative ideas. Because creativity is different across different studies and their domains, it's difficult to say which commonalities drive the relationship between the two.

If we know and accept the theory referred to as solipsism, which suggests that we don't really know if or what another person is thinking, and proposes that anything outside of one's own mind is uncertain, then grief as a research project is a philosophical conundrum. For example, am I alone in the universe, do other people think or do they even exist? – the argument then follows that the external world and what happens in other people's minds can't be known and might not exist outside of our own mind. It was impossible to know how other people were reacting to or dealing with Dom's death on the inside. In general, we know what grief is because we've read about other people's experience of it in poetry and memoirs. We know it's about loss. Even if we have felt prolonged grief, what we can't know exactly is what, or how, others are really feeling when they are grieving. There are very few visible and physical clues. In the past mourners wore black. How does a researcher or an author fill this gap in his understanding of the feelings and pain of grief? How can he convey the devastation of grief when the reader might not have experienced a loss?

On the other hand, grief answers one of the main ontological questions of existence and being. We know we exist when we grieve deeply for someone, not just because of the intense feelings experienced, but because we question that existence. Sometimes these feelings are so extreme they make some survivors think that they don't want to exist at all. They dread the thought of carrying on. For me and for those people still grieving, death is the closest we can get to the meaning of life. Existential anxiety is a common symptom that manifests itself during grief; I lost my self-worth and saw or felt no reason to carry on. There is also an existential crisis too with your identity. I noticed this happening also after Dom's death.

# Part 3 - Restoration (of Sorts)

For the first three years, the working title of this book was *Living in Shadow* because that's how grief feels: everything is overshadowed by loss, including loss of life and the loss of a future. In a sane moment, I imagined at the end of the process the work could be renamed *Leaving the Shadow*. I was told the grief would fade, so I assumed that's what it would feel like. That's what helpful people said it would be like. I would smile at the thought of remembering something funny Dominic had said or done. Perhaps at that point I would be able to write about him. Seeing him in photos would bring back that sense of pride I had in him, his achievements and his boyish good looks, instead of sadness. In the end, I didn't want Dominic's death to define my life; I wanted my life and my writing about him, creative or nonfiction, to reconcile his death and my reaction to it.

The world has always expressed itself creatively in death, and in grief. We only need to look at artefacts such as the pyramids in Egypt or the Step Pyramid of Djoser which used over eleven million cubic feet of stone and clay. The Taj Mahal, built by Shah Jahan in 1631, in memory of his wife, Mumtaz Mahal, taking over twenty years to complete. Even some of the smaller constructions such as Nelson's Column in central London, built to commemorate Nelson's death at the Battle of Trafalgar in 1805, are impressive. Nelson's statue alone is eighteen feet high, almost three and a half times the height of the man. All these artefacts and symbols show us how love and admiration for people can manifest itself through their loss. It's not a big leap to extend this architectural creativity through grief to the written word.

Even so, we all handle grief in our own time and space. In August 2019, nearly six years after Dom's death, Reuben took some flowers to Castle Sowerby church to visit his brother's grave for the first time since Dom's interment. In that moment, in my mind, Reuben stood taller than Nelson. The day was a significant milestone and a symbol of moving on with his own grief journey. For three years, Reuben had metaphorically remained on the backseat of the car as we drove down to Liverpool, confused, angry, not knowing why nor believing that his older brother was dead. He'd watched as his family disintegrated, first selling Vicargate, his home for seventeen years, then the family business. Reuben, like Dom and Chloe, was an integral part of running our two pubs, sometimes working a thirty-hour week while he was still at school.

After his A levels in 2016, Reuben was still in limbo; so he decided to take a year out. He couldn't understand what had happened to his bubble-wrapped country life. He picked the furthest destination he could find with snow and went to Japan to teach skiing. He fell in love with Japan, but couldn't stay at the end of the season, so he found an even-further-away place with snow and spent another year skiing in Mount Hotham, the powder snow capital of Victoria, Australia. He's now back in the UK studying Product Design in London.

Reuben left Hotham at the end of the ski season but didn't bring his ski kit back. He decided to tour Australia for a few months, meeting us for Christmas in Sydney. He thought he was going to return to Hotham to ski the following season, but he didn't. The huge ski bag came home with DHL in November 2019, two years later. Susan and I unpacked it as we Facetimed with him and he told us what to send to the charity shop and which items to keep. The latter included two pairs of skis, ski boots, a selection of base layers and three ski jackets, but not the out-of-date Snickers bar that we found in one of the pockets. I could see as we talked and held various items up to the phone, he had happy memories of his time away. A Hawaiian shirt brought a smile to his face, but a girl's mini skirt and pink jacket brought no recollection at all. Eventually there were two piles, the practical pile that we were keeping, and the other one. After his visit to Dom a few months earlier, he was sorting through his emotional baggage, and more so now with his ski kit. He was allowing himself to let go of the material things, just keeping the ones that made him smile. It seemed a good metaphor for him to relate to his dead brother, keep the happy memories, let the rest go.

When he was fifteen, Reuben wrote a song about his brother that he performed at the funeral. The writer Paulo Coelho reflects that every human being on this planet has at least one good story to tell his neighbour. Most people have the capacity to be creative, some more than others. Reuben has the capacity. He spent two years skiing, partying and burning both ends of the candle. The vast white space in which he was working, playing and teaching gave him the time and freedom to think about his grief too. He also had singing gigs in Japanese and Australian bars, so he spent two years writing songs and performing his grief. Loss and creativity seem to be key components of what it means to be human, so a link between the two should not come as a great surprise. The creative act, after all, is about reaching deep within oneself; it is a process that can be healing in that it enables us to express ourselves authentically and become more compassionate towards both ourselves and others.

Grief seems to be a fertile place from which to write or create. Your mind, your senses and your body are travelling to places they've never been. Sometimes you're in control; often you're not. You are experiencing emotions and a chemical explosion in your body that is beyond your comprehension. As the blood rushes through your veins, the chemicals dredged up by grief hit the left and right sides of your brain. I liken it to the mind-bending effects that the hallucinogens – such as LSD – had in the 1970s and '80s, but it's the grief that is intensifying your sensory perceptions, not the drug. As we grieve, we see and hear concomitant images all the time. We want to see our loved one alive, but they are no longer with us. Can these states exist at the same time? They certainly exist at the same time in our memory.

I write every day. It not only helps memorialising Dominic within various creative pieces, but it's helping me to refocus. Anyone who has suffered severe heartbreak after the death of someone close to them will have experienced the depth of pain that accompanies grief and will know that the grieving process is not to be taken lightly. Grieving is universal but distinctive to each person; however, what we may not associate with grieving is an awareness of freedom that may come with it – freedom from aspects of our pasts, freedom to create our futures. Accessing and engaging with our creativity is one way we can help ourselves or be helped to get through the grieving process.

# Death, Grief and Memoir

Memoir is an accessible vehicle that writers use to explore, expose and express their feelings. It acts as a productive displacement activity (Strobe and Shut, 1999). (Also, Freud if you recall over 100 years ago). It's also a medium that grievers use to answer the philosophical questions that follow a death. As you grieve you are desperate for information about why you are feeling that way. Memoir allows famous writers such as Barnes and Didion to explore and voice their feeling, reach a wide audience and then educate. As a result, their grief becomes accessible. It allows ordinary people like me to do the same. By sharing their work, these writers with a global reach have allowed me to reflect on what and why I've written about Dominic. It's their insights that have helped me to fine tune my own creativity. Despite this, by writing memoir, do writers write in order to save the memories of their loved ones, or to save themselves?

Hilary Mantel said in her essay on grief (Guardian, December 2014, para. 9), 'Recovery can seem like a betrayal. Passionately, you desire a way back to the lost object, but the only possible road, the road to life, leads away'. A road is one of the extended metaphors in *A Grief Observed*, by CS Lewis (1961). *A Grief Observed* captures the unpredictable, cyclical nature of mourning and Lewis's writing offers an extraordinarily coherent portrait of a mind in pain. Following the death of his wife, Lewis published the journal under the pseudonym NW Clerk and his name was only revealed after his death. Although he doesn't name his wife, he only refers to 'H', he wants her, and his time with her, narrated for posterity.

As the title suggests, he wanted to detach himself from her death and to act as a witness to the story as it unfolded. He also needed to encapsulate and describe how grief feels, and at the same time create her narrative so he didn't forget. His initial thoughts on doing this were to make a map of sorrow as a 'state'. He realised, however, that grief or sorrow isn't a state; it's a process and, instead of a map, it needs to be written as a history. Lewis argued (ibid.), 'there is something new to be chronicled every day'. Just as Julian Barnes became his wife's 'principal rememberer' I have for Dom, as well as aligning this memoir to Walter's assertions about creating a 'lasting memorial to the deceased'. I believe it to be one of the last steps in my grief management, enabling my mind to come to terms with Dom's death, even from a distance. Lewis noted his progress through this:

> What would H. herself think of this terrible little notebook to which I come back and back? Are these jottings morbid? ... I not only live each endless day in grief, but live each day thinking about living each day in grief. Do these notes merely aggravate that side of it? ... But what am I to do? I must have some drug, and reading isn't a strong enough drug now. By writing it all down ... I believe I get a little outside it. That's how I'd defend it to H. But ten to one she'd see a hole in the defence. (pp. 9–10)

Lewis is compelled to write about Helen and that is the drug. Reading isn't going to get him through the day. I experienced this addiction too. Writing about grief felt like a literary endorphin. Endorphins are a body's natural response to stress and anxiety. They act on the opiate receptors in our brains and reduce pain and boost pleasure, resulting in a feeling of well-being (BBC article, June 2016, para. 9). I found the more I wrote and explored, the more I wanted to write and understand. This was the same for Lewis as he went 'back and back' to his notebook, and questions whether 'H' would approve. He knew he needed to carry on through the mental fog and the forgetfulness that grief brings, as he struggled to remember how his wife looked: 'I have no photograph of her that's any good. I cannot even see her face distinctly in my imagination' (p. 15). Lewis was afraid that he might forget what his wife looked like. He wrote about meeting a man he hadn't seen in ten years, and how different the man was from how Lewis remembered him. He says, 'his actual presence ... was quite astonishingly different from the image I had carried with me (in my head) for those ten years. How can I hope that this will not happen to my memory of H.? That it is not happening already?' (pp. 19–20)

In her piece in the Guardian, Hilary Mantel writes:

> A Grief Observed is a lucid description of an obscure, muddled process, a process almost universal, one with no logic and no timetable. It is an honest attempt to write about aspects of the human and the divine which, he fears, 'won't go into language at all'.

Towards the end of her essay, Mantel pondered which shelf the book should sit on. Given Lewis's reputation, she assumed as I did, that it would be 'religion'. However, she pointed out that the people who would benefit from it could also potentially be running away from God. She also recommended that it shouldn't sit in the 'self-help' section because, she lamented, there are no 'cheering anecdotes.' I too reflected on this; grief memoir is a growing and successful genre but Mantel's comments made me consider where I would place the memoir of a sad dad.

For Lewis grief is 'like a long valley, a winding valley where any bend may reveal a totally new landscape' (p. 29). The love story between him and his wife lasted about four years and was made into a feature film called 'Shadowlands' (1993). The film is set in 1952 at Magdalen College where Lewis taught between 1925 and 1954. The last scene after Joy's death shows Anthony Hopkins, who plays Lewis in the film, wandering down a long winding path. The valley stretches before him out of sight and out of shot. In an earlier scene, where Joy visits him at the cottage he shares with his brother, she notices a picture on the wall, which is also of a valley, and comments how beautiful it is. He explains it's the Golden Valley in Hertfordshire, and he has happy memories of it as a child. This valley is important to Lewis and his childhood, and as Joy becomes important to him, they go to find it together. It becomes a shared memory.

In 'Shadowlands', there's another early scene where Lewis (Hopkins) is tutoring a student in his private quarters. Lewis asks the boy, who he caught stealing a book from a bookshop, why he reads. The student says, 'We read to know we are not alone.'

I was surprised by his response, as was Lewis, who later used the line in one of his lectures. It's important to know about other people and to read their stories; it's part of the human condition. I would take this further, suggesting that we write down our memories of the dead so that we, at least, know they are not alone or forgotten, and if those memories are shared, other readers can get to know them too.

It's hard not to reflect on Lewis without thinking about the many other giants of literature who came before or after him at Oxford. These include, amongst others, favourites of mine: Percy Shelley, Oscar Wilde and JRR Tolkien, and two poets who survived Lewis, Robert Graves and John Betjeman (whom Lewis taught but didn't get on with). I also couldn't ignore a simple but beautiful plaque on the college wall that commemorates the two hundred and thirteen alumni who were killed during the First World War. The plaque led me to a website called 'The Slow Dusk', which reflects on the lives of all the young men who died, and what these war dead may have achieved had they not died, and what the world may have lost. I often reflect on this too about Dom. Sometimes I'm a bit selfish and wonder about grandchildren, but mainly I agonise about what he possibly could have done with his life and what he would be doing now at the age of thirty. I'm pleased that Dom and his friends didn't have to experience anything like the First World War. I've watched them move on with their lives and assume the responsibilities of husbands, fathers, house owners or all three. Dom wasn't a polymath; he didn't have a magnum opus waiting to be published posthumously. It's not what the world has lost, but certainly what he, his family and friends have.

The name of the 'Slow Dusk' site comes from a poem written by Wilfred Owen (1893–1918), who, although not an alumnus of Oxford, wrote 'Anthem for Doomed Youth' (Appendix 9), which is about young people like the Oxford 1912 and 1913 cohorts, miles from home. For them death came quickly and noisily:

— Only the monstrous anger of the guns, only the stuttering rifles' rapid rattle' (line 3), and often even without time for prayers or bells. 'And each slow dusk a drawing-down of blinds' (line 14).

This was a further reminder that, in an instant, Dom's life was lost too.

# A Creative Writer's Approach to Death

You may have wondered why I gave Eminem as much weight as CS Lewis? There are a number of reasons for this, including personal, academic and cultural ones. As actors in grief narratives, we have different relationships that bind us: CS Lewis and Joy, husband and wife; Eminem and Proof, two men who have grown up together; Ian and Dominic, father and son. This begs the question, have we grieved in the same ways for our loved ones? It's not a question I began with; it only came about as I started to read other people's grief stories, poems or songs. However, in the world of art, I suspect Lewis and Eminem are just as 'weighty' as each other, clearly for different reasons. From a personal perspective, Eminem was Dom's hero.

*A Grief Observed*, for example, is an object of serious study and the go-to reference book for any student or scholar of grief or loss. There is a reason for this, which I discussed in part two. For my research and in complete contrast to the literary canon that is CS Lewis, I chose 'Difficult' because it too depicts a man, hurting and lost. I also wanted to include other forms of grief narrative in the memoir, and this song was written by a contemporary songwriter and from a genre of which I had little experience. I also thought it would be interesting to juxtapose two giants in their fields, but complete opposites in every other sense.

On the first reading of 'Difficult', the metaphors, the descriptions of the aftermath following Proof's death and the feelings of the writer were expressed humbly and simply. I didn't have to dig them out. This song wasn't aimed at academics, highbrow readers or listeners. It was aimed at kids like Dom. Even though the street language is a fundamental part of its structure, which I needed to pick my way through, the words are simple, almost childlike. Like poetry, lyrics need to cram a lot into their message. However, unlike a poem, there are no flowery images or symbols in a rap piece between a dead friend and a singer who wants to grieve in the violent and macho world that is rap. Consequently, the impact Proof's death had on the rapper is there for all to see. Eminem's reflections are from his heart. I did have to Google an urban dictionary to see what 'G' meant (Gangster), but I didn't have to watch a film to get further under the skin of their relationship as I did with 'Shadowlands'. The visceral emotion is there in those simple lyrics.

There is a world of difference between the cultures of Lewis and Eminem, but does that mean they grieve differently? It needs no explanation, but from an emotional perspective, Lewis lost his wife of four years and Eminem a lifelong male friend. It begs a further question: do relationships attract a 'grade' or a level of grief appropriate to or based on the length of the relationship, the type of relationship we have with the deceased or the sex of the griever or the deceased? I can't answer those questions as I have never lost my wife or a childhood friend, and this book didn't necessarily set out to address grief of that kind. The language, tone, narrative arc and the aesthetic that are found in Lewis and Eminem reflect, in a creative way, the deep loss and pain that we feel for the person we have lost. In order to give the reader a profounder level of understanding of our emotions, to try to explain to the reader the depth of our despair, writers scour the darkest recesses of their creative selves to find literary comparisons, metaphors, allegories and similes. It's impossible. Nevertheless, as Barnes, Didion, MacDonald and Riley show us, we can only tell the reader our emotional reality. When we write from that perspective, it's about expressing the voice of your heart rather than the voice in your head. When sharing our emotional truth, it's important to share what you think, as opposed to what others want to hear.

No matter how detached I try to be, I can't escape the elegiac nature of the subject and how it has shaped my creative work. At times, pathos dominates the narrative, and nervous non sequiturs expose my imposter syndrome. It's inevitable that when the creative writer creates, the instinct is to make the narrative as sympathetic to a reader as possible, especially if they have had the same experience. When your child dies, so does your ability to find metaphors that can fully capture your grief. Using writing as a therapeutic tool to rewrite your self-narrative can bring a fresh perspective to bridging the gap between grieving and the despair.

As I near the completion of the book, I realise that I now have serious responsibilities as a writer, more so as an academic autoethnographer. This memoir is about Dominic, but it is also about loss and how that leads to creativity and the hope for an alternative future without him. I know I cannot write a narrative about him without a critical evaluation, or open up my personal life to an audience without critique. I also cannot assume, but I hope, the reader will recognise the need or value of my work to others who experience a similar loss and the same emotional issues.

Grief is the response to death. It's only there because of love. Depression, meaning-making and eventually resolution allow us to come to terms with death. In the books, poems and lyrics discussed here and in my response to Dom's death, I can see some of those recovery signs. Joan Didion eventually recognised that she couldn't have saved John's life, and Eminem wanted to support Proof's widow. Strobe's *Dual Process model* (1999) highlights that grief is an evolving process, the attachments to your loved one are slowly let go and your thoughts move to your life without them.

In the centre of your grief, you are not necessarily aware that your life is trying to repair itself (Neimeyer, 2013). But you are aware you are trying to reconstruct the bond with your loved one, rather than leaving it behind. I would argue that you are also trying to maintain relational continuity (Degroot, 2012), but you're unaware how that can be achieved. Throughout my memoir, my own journey unconsciously mirrored many of the same morbid scenes that I'd read in these other books. I asked myself similar philosophical questions to those posed by other writers and I felt similar reactions to the grief that they wrote about.

In my memoir and its analysis, I've used an anthropological perspective wisely, exploring social and cultural norms, how death has been viewed historically, and more importantly how people have written about the death of their loved ones, especially 'in memoriam'. Seven years later I'm offered, like many of the writers before me, an experience which at the right moment can be transported into a creative work. Telling personal stories about Dom and about my grief publicly and honestly, will always carry personal, relationship and ethical risks. Some may even question my morality, indeed my sanity, but those risks are worth taking. The story needs to be told, the research needs to be taken further, but as Butler (2005) writes, our willingness to risk ourselves – our stories, our identities, our commitments – in relation to others constitutes our very chance of becoming human (p. 136).

# Why?

As a creative writer, I've tried to embrace the unimaginable and uncharted world that I have been occupying for several years. I wrote endlessly at the time of Dominic's death, and like Robinson Crusoe when, months later, eventually exploring the confines of his new world, I discovered those narrative footprints in the sand. I didn't recognise them as mine at first; I started to wonder who else was inhabiting my island. As I analyse those early footprints in my writing, I realise they are 'steps' in a recovery process; creative writing was indeed therapeutic, and that my research was now closer to art than science.

There is in my mind, and perhaps in yours too as a reader, a final gnawing question that I've failed to understand or address. Have I been writing about Dominic and the future life he has lost, or, have I been a narcissist right from the very beginning, and the book is about me?

> If we don't change the direction we are headed, we will end up where we are going. (Lau Tzu, also known as Laozi or Lao-Tze, c. 500 BC)

I am not a clinician, philosopher or psychologist, just a sad dad. This memoir was only written because of Dom's death. It wouldn't exist if he hadn't been in that car on that night. But he was. Now I can see that writing was part of the healing process and it was how I processed my grief. It was however important to view it through an introspective biographical lens. By doing this, Dom's memoir might become a source of inspiration, an elixir of healing and hope for readers to confront their own grief and find strength in family bonds. The profound lesson that emerges from this tragedy is the importance of cherishing every moment and never taking the ones we love for granted.

The answer to my unanswered question and indeed my conclusions, can only be measured by my own experience of grief; and constrained or magnified by the love for my son and my response to his death. Against all the odds and logic, he will now be memorialised because his death changed my life by discovering writing as a therapy, which has allowed me to write about his.

# Dominic – My Son

There is a dichotomy with Dominic, a 'yin and yang' with the two opposing sides to his persona. On one hand, for me as a parent, a colleague and a friend, he was what they call in the corporate world 'an impact player'. He made things happen. He knew what was needed to get things done. People gravitated to him for help and advice. His phone never stopped ringing or buzzing as texts came in. They knew he was capable, and just as important they knew he would make himself available to help them. He grew in strength, stature and intellect over the last four years of his life. The pupil became the master.

On the other hand, he didn't seem to be aware of his abilities, capabilities, his personal qualities or his good looks. I think that was part of his charm, and I love him for that.

One of the most difficult things in coming to terms with the death of someone you love is that the world remains the same for everyone else; the earth continues to spin, the birds continue to sing, the grass still grows and the kettle still boils despite that person not being here. I have realised that the strength and inspiration I seek is through Dominic, his actions, his absolute selflessness and of course my memory of him. I take pride, hope and inspiration from all the good and kind things that people have reminded us about him, in cards and letters. I also take inspiration from the unassuming way he lived his life.

I've looked everywhere for inspiration and guidance to try to make sense of it all. I've read books, papers and research from psychologists, philosophers, theorists and authors, some of them discussed in this book. I read Carol Anne

Duffy, poet Laureate. Her book *Love Poems* (2010) is a slim volume of fifty-five pages. As confessional poets do, it's all about 'me'; it's all about hand wringing and unrequited or lost love, but in it I saw a glimpse of someone else in pain. One week after Dom's death, Reuben and I met another author, Stephen McClintock, who was selling his book in Waterstones. He lost his brother in a car crash when he was twenty-five, and has since lived his life and written books in his brother's memory. Twenty years later, he speaks with pride about his brother, and says his brother's memory was instrumental to his success. And then to the other extreme of searching for help, a bottle of red wine, several – French, Italian, Chilean or Spanish – it didn't matter but it dulled the pain. There was no guidance or inspiration from them.

The two years before Dom died, I encouraged him to emigrate to Canada. Whilst he listened and understood my argument of a 'better' life, I knew deep down that he wasn't interested. He was happy with his life, and he loved his friends and family too much to leave them behind. We won't ever know which direction Dominic's life was heading in and if at twenty-two he had got to where he was destined to be. What I do know is that he touched the lives and hearts of everyone he met on his way. And now in his death, I hope he may have changed the direction that some of us are heading in, for the better. I hope younger people will drive their cars more slowly. I hope older people will be more reflective and perhaps in some small way follow Dominic's example of just enjoying the simple things, and enjoying life for what it is.

In grief we look for answers; the question is often Why? Why him? Why us? Why me? Throughout 2014, 2015 and at the start of 2016, I wrote reflexively, simply writing down what was in my head and heart at that moment. Sometimes, in the early days I was so out of my mind, I couldn't remember what I'd written. In other more lucid times, I was able to digitally zoom in on human behaviour and our cultural response to death. As I experienced them, I acknowledged the variations of the five stages of grief; 'Loss and Avoidance', 'Oscillation and Confrontation', and 'Restoration (of Sorts)' are the main chapter headings of this book and are loosely based on them. At the time of writing (2023), the one thing I disagree with Kübler Ross and all the other theorists on is the eventual acceptance of the situation.

Certainly, for me, I know Dom is dead, but I can't accept it. I understand he is no longer flesh and blood and we need to adjust our lives to make the pain more bearable; I still can't accept it. We are more concerned about keeping our loved ones' memory alive than about ourselves. Eventually I concluded that I needed to create a feeling of Dom's immortality in the face of his biological death (Toynbee, 1963, 1976; Lifton, 1967; Shneidman, 1976).

Without exception, in all the grief memoir I've read, the authors strive to achieve it for their loved ones in their work. In real life, our own immortality can be achieved in several ways, the first being through our children. If you believe as Saunders writes in *Lincoln in the Bardo*, immortality could be through the release to a higher form of life, and then to be reborn to a new life. Finally, it can also be through our own creative works.

Dominic died too early and through no fault of his own. This makes me aware of my own mortality and more importantly Susan's, Chloe's and Reuben's. No matter how much I wish Dom was in the bardo waiting for me to join him there, there is no afterlife. Allegorically, after his death, I believe as a victim and survivor of grief, there can be a rebirth of sorts. I have discussed this and 'a different normal' with other survivors; consequently, I put the level of normality we can achieve down to individual grit and determination to survive. One of the key influencers in recovery, one that is never discussed, can be our sheer inner strength and belief in ourselves. The well-meaning, even from the trained supporters around us who think they're helping, are often lacking the experience or real knowledge about death. On that basis, if you can escape Janus and his two faces, you are in control of your own rebirth - but you need to survive your grief. Nevertheless, I know I will never see Dom in the bardo, so for me, the only immortality option left is my creativity. Our literary DNA.

I wrote earlier, when Dom was born and we brought him home for the first time, I said to Susan as I looked in the rear-view mirror, 'You do realise we've got a baby in the back of the car? What do we do now?'

We had no idea how to take care of our three-day-old, helpless new-born. There wasn't a 'manual', there wasn't a helpdesk with an 0800 number and Google hadn't been invented yet.

We just became the best parents that we could be.

When he died, I whispered again to Susan, 'What do we do now?' I can still vividly picture him twenty-two years earlier, seated in his child's car seat and reflected in the rear-view mirror of our car. But now, I imagine him upside down, dying in the back of a BMW after it had smashed into a wall. Today, we're the helpless ones. I've exhausted Google for over eight years looking for answers, and who would answer my cries of pain even if there was a helpdesk – God?

In some respects, we are the lucky ones. We have unbreakable bonds with Chloe and Reuben and we all have our personal and collective memories of Dom. Like John James who wrote the *Grief Recovery Method* to help himself and others in the 1970s, this book also serves as a first-hand, self-styled 'self-help' manual of sorts.

But most importantly, I've kept my promise to Dom and his friends by creating a book of memories of him. In doing so, I've also given him digital dignity in death, and allowed him his digital immortality.

IP Loftus

# End Matter

# How Important are our Photos?

> Essentially the camera makes everyone a tourist in other people's reality, and eventually in one's own. — Susan Sontag (p. 60)

In this memoir I reference photos or photography dozens of times. One of the books discussed, *Levels of Life* (2013) by Julian Barnes, has photography as a main thread running through it. Without doubt, especially now when most people have a smartphone in their pocket, photography is an accessible and important part of everyone's life. In our house, we have walls filled with photos of our three children going back thirty years, but since his death, there are now many more of Dominic.

In her book *On Photography* (2002), Susan Sontag discusses the philosophical question of how reality may be perceived and knowledge gained through photography, but she also reviews photography in its context as a tool, an industry and an activity. To take a photograph, Sontag writes, 'is to appropriate the thing photographed' (p. 2). The appropriation, the stealing without touching, the having a semblance of knowledge, she likens to perversion. Sontag claims everything is gist to the camera, and in the end, no matter what the photographer may want, everything becomes equal in value so long as it makes an interesting picture.

Like many of the personal sections in this book, Sontag's essays are meditations and ruminations on various themes. In Sontag's case, photography and photographic images play an ambiguous but potent force in modern consciousness. As a father taking photos of our three children, it never crossed my mind to think about the philosophy of photography. My only objective was to capture images of the kids as they grew up. They are memories for the children to recall happy times, and we look at them together occasionally to reminisce. In the future, we would show them to our children's children and wonder which of our grandchildren looked like their mum or dad just as we had ruminated over our parents' photographs.

Sontag's collection of six essays and quotations is not a book for a photographic beginner like me. It is an attempt at a sweeping critique of everything photographic, aimed at those wanting to venture into the philosophical world of photography. In addressing an array of topics in the field, Sontag speaks from a wide cultural, literary, historical and philosophical background and expects the reader to have familiarity with all of these areas. Her commentary ranges widely from a detailed analysis of individual photographers to why people fear having their photographs taken, from historical development in photographic equipment to why people take pictures of any and everything, from tourist to scientist, from artist to technician, from surveillance photography to medical examinations.

Her main debate, however, revolves around whether photography is an art form or a tool. This deliberation weaves its way in and out of her essays. It reminds me of the argument I had with myself when thinking about Dom's death and writing creatively about him. Can I write about my dead son in an artistic or creative way without being too maudlin or narcissistic? It was this measured consideration that drew me to Sontag's book, and it gave me a different perspective when I thought about the psychological impact of inserting photos of Dom in this work. Occasionally with a sibling, Dom appears as an apparition or a haunting reminder to me over these pages. Sontag insists that taking a photo is uncompromising and puts reality on pause. It denies a connection and continuity, and confers on each moment the character of a mystery. As an onlooker, or in this case a writer, this might be true, but as the photographer or a participant in my photo, I recall how the pictures were taken in the moment, with love. Whilst some might look enigmatic, their time, location and their characters are obvious to me. Seeing my dead son again as I looked at each photo for insertion in this memoir felt like a punch. The photos cannot tell the whole truth; that can only come from my words and narration.

To know someone or a place by seeing a photo is to know it as a distanced, almost recycled fragmentary scene. When the children were born, I wasn't aware of that, but today, I feel only too keenly how photography is a way to remember Dom at a specific time and place, and to explore my inner self as I ask, 'Have I led a good life and will the world be a better place when I've gone?' This questioning or discovery is not accidental. As we grieve, we can only make that discovery when we are ready to let go and accept our loss.

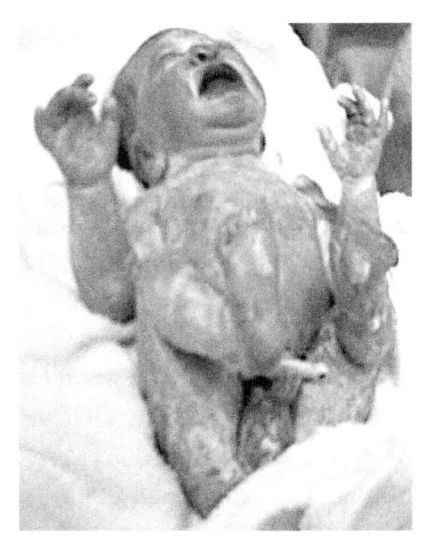

My discovery begins with the photos of a son, taken at three minutes old, still covered in vernix caseosa, a proud father holding his first-born son or of a young man holding his glass of beer in front of the campervan that he's just renovated.

It begins with that which matters to you. It is not our eyes the camera satisfies, but our mind. A photo is a visual statement that tells the viewer what matters to you about these things or those people. It's more instant than a memoir.

Sontag's third essay, 'Melancholy Objects' (p. 53–p.89) and her descriptions of the 'diligent hunter-with-a-camera' (p. 57) made the link for me with my photographer and writer selves after Dom's death. As a photographer, I stepped back and became 'an observer'. Sontag's book describes the work of several photographers, flaneurs such as Paul Martin and Arnold Genthe in the 1890s, who also stepped back and took snapshots of the shabby streets of London and China town in San Francisco respectively. This allowed me to draw a narrative comparison with George Orwell's work such as *Down and Out in Paris and London* (1933) and *The Road to Wigan Pier* (1937). Sontag, however, spends much of the essay discussing the impact of the surrealists on photography, highlighting that the biggest thing they misunderstood was time itself.

She goes on to say that what makes a photo surreal is its undeniable tragedy as a message from time past. That hit a very raw nerve. The important thing for me was Sontag exposing photography as the most simplistic of the mimetic arts. It allowed me to link Martin and Genthe to literary giants like Orwell and it gave me the courage to include photos of Dom here in this book, as a fragile testament to a lost son.

# About the Author

Tragedy struck when Ian's eldest son, Dom, lost his life in a car accident caused by a drunk driver on October 4th, 2013. This devastating event shook Ian to his core. Amidst the grief and despair, Ian found solace in writing. He believes that without his family and the healing power of writing, he might not have made it to this point where you now hold his book.

Following Dom's death, Ian completed a Ph.D. in Writing. His doctoral thesis focused into the therapeutic use of creative and self-expressive as a therapy to help deal with trauma, particularly grief.

The death of a child before its parents is against the natural order of things. It leaves countless questions unanswered in a parent's mind. For Ian, writing provided an outlet to express and explore these overwhelming thoughts. Throughout his Ph.D. research, he documented his actions, experiences and the ruminations of a grieving father. The result was a poignant personal memoir entitled *Smiler*. 68,000 words of honesty and raw emotion.

Having spent ten years in academia researching grief, Ian brings a wealth of knowledge to this book, his extensive research has contributed to its depth and authenticity.

www.ianploftus.com

# Acknowledgements

Following the untimely death of Dominic, my eldest son, one thing I finally learned about grief and depression is not to surround myself with pills and potions but instead, keep creative company. So, I give my heartfelt thanks to Liverpool John Moores University Screen School and especially my MA and Ph.D. cohort. They helped me keep my finger off the self-destruct button during my research and thankfully kept me functioning after that fateful day on the 3rd October 2013.

To Prof. Catherine Cole, Associate Dean, Director of Studies, author, mentor and thankfully a Pommy lover, Conan Leavey and Dr Jackie Newton, who gave me lots to think about and lots of encouragement.

To James Friel, author, mentor, all round good guy and bon vivant.

To Sean Dick, who guided me to the latest academic thinking on grief that strengthened my resolve.

A big thank you to David and Karen Pitty, who camped in our paddock for two months to be close by. Later, for allowing me to use their house when I needed space to write. And huge thanks to Nicola and Gus Benn, who brought hot food and support to our house every day for six months.

To my family, Susan, Chloe and Reuben. There are actually no words…

And to Dominic. This work wouldn't exist without you. I wrote a few poems about you when you were alive, but after you died, I've written tens of thousands of words in an attempt to keep my memory from fading. I can only dream that they do our journey together some justice, with the hope it may give another grieving parent courage and will guide other survivors through their bereavement in some small way.

Finally, about 530,000 people die in the UK every year. Hidden among that number there are 6,500 suicides and 7,000 people killed in road traffic accidents. However, most of the deceased, regardless of the cause, will have a loved one left behind and grieving for them. It's to them my work is dedicated. Us, the survivors.

# Appendices

# Appendix 1 Thoughts on a Cumbrian Lad at Bowscale Tarn

Even with lashing wind,
Bowscale Tarn is flat,
protected,
Carrock on my right, Combe
and Knott to the front.
A Facebook fact,
Dominic and Luce often made this hike,
I hear him call her to heel despite the howling easterly gale.
His voice,
a thousand times sharper than the biting air,
slices to my heart,
my chest,
gossamer thin,
is no protection.
The water, black, bottomless as the myth tells,
somewhere,
two immortal fish,
one given the power of speech.

At the water's edge I'm drawn to its limitlessness.
In my insanity I call the fish to heel,
again, then again.
I step out
      to the first exposed stone, I'm free.
Against the squall, I call, the fish yet again.
I scan the water for a sign and step,
                to
the next visible stone.

Now a foot on each, the water,
still, now invites me,

I
  try
    to
      fathom
         its
            depth.

A Wordsworth poem bounces around the fell,
(or in my head?)
The Cumbrian accent slices to my heart.

'And both the undying fish that swim,
through Bowscale-Tarn did wait on him,
the pair were servants of his eye in their immortality,
they moved about in open sight,
to and fro, for his delight'.
                                      One more step.

There
  are
    no
      more
        stones
        to step to
The storm has dropped,
Wordsworth has stopped.
I could dive into the warm blankness,
and hold onto the tail of the immortal fish,
swim to eternity, to

the bottom that doesn't exist.
I won't hear his voice again,
only the immortal talking fish.

# Appendix 2  Surprised by Joy

Surprised by joy—impatient as the Wind
I turned to share the transport—Oh! with whom
But Thee, long buried in the silent Tomb,
That spot which no vicissitude can find?
Love, faithful love, recalled thee to my mind—
But how could I forget thee?—Through what power,
Even for the least division of an hour,
Have I been so beguiled as to be blind
To my most grievous loss!—That thought's return
Was the worst pang that sorrow ever bore,
Save one, one only, when I stood forlorn,
Knowing my heart's best treasure was no more;
That neither present time, nor years unborn
Could to my sight that heavenly face restore.

# Appendix 3 On my First Son

Farewell, thou child of my right hand, and joy;
My sin was too much hope of thee, lov'd boy.
Seven years tho' wert lent to me, and I thee pay,
Exacted by thy fate, on the just day.
O, could I lose all father now! For why
Will man lament the state he should envy?
To have so soon 'scap'd world's and flesh's rage,
And if no other misery, yet age?
Rest in soft peace, and, ask'd, say, 'Here doth lie
Ben Jonson his best piece of poetry.'
For whose sake henceforth all his vows be such,
As what he loves may never like too much.

# Appendix 4 The Dash (1996) – by Linda Ellis

I read of a man who stood to speak
at the funeral of a friend.
He referred to the dates on the tombstone
from the beginning…to the end.

He noted that first came the date of birth
and spoke the following date with tears,
but he said what mattered most of all
was the dash between those years.

For that dash represents all the time
that they spent alive on earth.
And now only those who loved them
know what that little line is worth.

For it matters not, how much we own,
the cars…the house…the cash.
What matters is how we live and love
and how we spend our dash.

So, think about this long and hard.
Are there things you'd like to change?
For you never know how much time is left
that can still be rearranged.

If we could just slow down enough
to consider what's true and real
and always try to understand
the way other people feel.

And be less quick to anger
and show appreciation more
and love the people in our lives
like we've never loved before.

If we treat each other with respect
and more often wear a smile,
remembering that this special dash
might only last a little while.

So, when your eulogy is being read,
with your life's actions to rehash…
would you be proud of the things they say
about how you spent YOUR dash.

# Appendix 5 The One I need the Most

It is terribly unfair
the one person I need
to help face this crisis
is now dead and gone.

She would have known
The advice I need now
To try and survive this
But she's dead, gone.

There is no blame now
You were not to know
That I would need you
soon as you were gone.

# Appendix 6  My Friend

Thinking of you every day
again…
and again
but even in my thoughts of
hope
nothing stops the pain.

Words I cannot speak
The things that have changed
Who saw it happening?
Now we're here.
… A barrier
Or a hole
An emptiness deep inside, a horrible gap
That's
Dark and sincere.

So close- yet
So far away.
Kept to a place
you will forever stay.

I will live until our meeting day.

Not in reach
Cannot touch
But quietly listening out for us-
As we are for you…
Always.

# Appendix 7 Hope is the Thing with Feathers

Hope is the thing with feathers -
That perches in the soul -
And sings the tune without the words -
And never stops - at all -
And sweetest - in the Gale - is heard -
And sore must be the storm -
That could abash the little Bird
That kept so many warm -
I've heard it in the chillest land -
And on the strangest Sea -
Yet - never - in Extremity,
It asked a crumb - of me.

# Appendix 8 Difficult

(Warning, there is some explicit language…)

Verse 1

They ask me am I okay, they ask me if I'm happy
Are they asking me that because of the shit that's been thrown at me?
Or am I just a little snappy and they genuinely care?
Doody, most of my life it's just been me and you there
And I continuously stare at pictures of you
I never got to say I love you as much as I wanted to, but I do
Yeah, I say it now when you can't hear me
What the fuck good does that do me now?
But somehow I know you're near me in presence
Oh, I went and dropped some presents off for Easter
To them two little beautiful boys of yours to try to ease their
Minds a little, and dog, you'll never believe this
But Sharonda actually talks to me now — Jesus!
And everyone else is just tryin' to pick up the pieces
Man, how could you touch so many fuckin' lives and just leave us?
They say grievance has a way of affectin' everyone different
If it's true, how the fuck I'm s'posed to get over you?
Difficult as it sounds

Chorus

Doody, I drop a tear in a rhyme
The day you find it is the day I stop missin' DeShaun
Holton, it was written, it was woven
For a soldier to leave so suddenly — got me wide open
How could God take a soul so dope and
Turn around, leave us all heartbroken?

Know that you're sayin', Keep goin'! Be a man! No emotion!'
It's your duty, until we meet again, Doody

Verse 2

'Doody' — that's what we'd call each other
I don't know where it came from
But it just stuck with us; we was always brothers
Never thought about each other's skin colors
'Til one day we was walkin' up the block in the summer
It was like 90 degrees, I was catchin' a sunburn
Tryin' to walk under the trees just to give me some comfort
I'm moanin', I just wanna get home and
I look over, and your shirt is off I'm like, 'You're gonna fry,' you're like,
'No, I won't I'm black, stupid! And black people, they got melatonin
In their skin — we don't burn,' meanwhile my face is glowin'
And I feel like I'm on fire And the entire time you're just laughin' at me
And snappin' at me with your shirt, bastard
And I still have to get you back for that shit
And by the way, them Playboy rings my mother stole from you
Well, Nate finally got 'em back, shit It must've been at least sixteen years ago
Well, I put 'em in your cask— oww
Movin' past it, it still ain't registered yet
But you can bet, your legacy they'll never forget
The Motor City, Motown, hip hop vet Hip Hop Shop, dreads, it don't stop there
Yeah, as difficult as it sounds

Chorus

Doody, I drop a tear in a rhyme
The day you find it is the day I stop missin' DeShaun

Holton, it was written, it was woven
For a soldier to leave so suddenly — got me wide open
How could God take a soul so dope and
Turn around, leave us all heartbroken?
Know that you're sayin', 'Keep goin'! Be a man! No emotion!'
It's your duty, until we meet again, Doody

Verse 3

And this might sound a little strange, but I'ma tell it
I found that jacket that you left at my wedding
And I picked it up to smell it
I wrapped it up in plastic until I put it in glass
And hang up in the hallway so I can always look at it
And as for all me and D12 we feel like 'Fuck rap!'
It feels like our general just fuckin' died in our lap
We shut off all our pagers, all our cell numbers is changed
Our two-ways are in the trash
So some cats will have to find a new way
And I know it feels like the dreams will die with you today
But the truth is they're all still here, and you ain't
Purple Gang, you gotta keep pressin' on
Don't ever give up the dream, dog, I got love for you all
And Doody, it's true you brought people together
Who never woulda been in the same room if it wasn't for you
You were the peacemaker, Doody
I know sometimes you were moody
But you hated confrontation and truly hated the feuding
But you was down for yours whenever it came to scrappin'
If it had to happen, it had to happen
    Believe me, I know you're the one who taught me to throw them
  bows back on Dresden
From eggin' cars to paintballin' and gettin' arrested

To sittin' across from each other in cells, laughin' and jestin'
They tried to hit us for five years for that, no question
    I guess them hookers and bums that we shot up didn't show up for
   court, so we got off on a technicality, left sweatin'
Me, you and… what's his face? I forgot his fuckin' name
Shame he even came to your funeral, he betrayed our team
And if I see him again I'ma punch him in the fuckin' face
And that's on Hailie Jade, Whitney Laine and Alaina's name
I'll let the pistol bang once just to lick a shot
In the air for you, and pour some liquor out
With Obie in the parking lot of 54 just before
We were supposed to get in cars to come and see you once more
Difficult as it sounds

Doody!

# Appendix 9 More Than a Sonnet.

Before I know it, you're six, missing teeth,
and legs stretching beyond belief.
I hardly recognise that porcelain face,
that toothless smile seems out of place.

What's happened since Iraq invaded,
a blond, and engaging laugh pervaded,
chattering sibling, fighting for attention,
summer house, a Christmas Child, family perfection?

I never seem to find the time,
for important things like nursery rhyme,
double cuddles, tucked up tight,
football, tennis, or your fluttering kite.
But I offer; single occupancy and shoes,
first hand clothes, religion and news.
I'll also give, hidden culture and Vicargate,
security, I'll fight naivety and negotiate.
Even now, I check to see if you still breathe,
I touch your head, extinguish the light, and leave.

# Appendix 10 Anthem for Doomed Youth

What passing-bells for these who die as cattle?
    — Only the monstrous anger of the guns.
    Only the stuttering rifles' rapid rattle
Can patter out their hasty orisons.
No mockeries now for them; no prayers nor bells;
    Nor any voice of mourning save the choirs,—
The shrill, demented choirs of wailing shells;
    And bugles calling for them from sad shires.

What candles may be held to speed them all?
    Not in the hands of boys, but in their eyes
Shall shine the holy glimmers of goodbyes.
    The pallor of girls' brows shall be their pall;
Their flowers the tenderness of patient minds,
And each slow dusk a drawing-down of blinds.

# Bibliography

Barnes, J. (2008) *Nothing to be Frightened of.* London: Jonathan Cape.

Barnes, J. (2013) *Levels of Life.* London: Jonathan Cape.

Bhabha, H.K. (1990) *Nation and Narration.* New York, NY: Routledge & Keegan Paul.

Bhabha, H.K. (1994) *The Location of Culture.* London: Routledge.

Byatt, A.S. (1996) *Babel Tower.* Colchester, Essex: Vintage.
AS Byatt, in *Possession: A Romance* (1990), AS Byatt, in *Possession: A Romance* (1990),
Carson, S. (2012) *Your Creative Brain: Seven Steps to Maximize Imagination, Productivity, and Innovation in Your Life.* Hoboken, NJ: Jossey-Bass.

Chang, H. (2008) *Autoethnography as Method.* New York, NY: Routledge.

Coetzee, J.M. (2015) *Diary of a Bad Year.* New York, NY: Vintage.

Didion, J. (2015) *The Year of Magical Thinking.* London: Harper Collins.

Duffy, C.A. (2010) *Love Poems.* London: Pan Macmillan.

Freud, S. (1957) Mourning and melancholia. In: Strachey, J. (ed. and tr.) *The Standard Edition of the Complete Psychological Works of Sigmund Freud 14.* [online] London: Hogarth Press, pp. 273–300. Available at: https://www.scirp.org/(S(lz5mqp453edsnp55rrgjct55))/reference/referencespapers.aspx?referenceid=495038 (Accessed 11 June 2017)

Feuerbach, L (1841) *The Essence of Christianity* Leipzig, Germany: Otto Wigand

Holman Jones, S., Adams, T.E. and Ellis, C. (2013) *Handbook of Autoethnography*. [online] Washington, DC: Taylor & Francis, p. 10. Available through **https://www.amazon.co.uk/Kindle-eBooks**

Holman Jones, S., Adams, T.E. and Ellis, C. (2013) *Handbook of Autoethnography*. [online] Washington, DC: Taylor & Francis, pp. 19–20. Available through **https://www.amazon.co.uk/Kindle-eBooks**

Hughes, T. (1970) *Crow. Life and Songs of the Crow.* London: Faber and Faber.

James, W. (1890) *The Principles of Psychology*. New York: Henry Holt.

Jamison, K. (1993) *Touched with Fire: Manic-depressive Illness and the Artistic Temperament*. New York, NY: Free Press.

Klass, D., Silverman, P.R. and Nickman, S.L. (eds.) (1996) *Continuing Bonds: New Understandings of Grief*. Washington, DC: Taylor & Francis.

Kübler-Ross, E. (1969) *On Death and Dying*. New York, NY: Macmillan.

Lewis, C.S. (1961) *A Grief Observed*. London: Faber and Faber.

Ludwig, A.M. (1995) *The Price of Greatness: Resolving the Creativity and Madness Controversy*. New York, NY: Guilford.

McDonald, H. (2014) *H is for Hawke*. London: Jonathan Cape.

Menninger, K. (1956) *Man Against Himself*. Boston, MA: Mariner Books.

Muncey, T. (2010) *Creating Autoethnographies*. Thousand Oaks, CA: Sage Publishing.

Neimeyer, R.A. and Mahoney, M.J. (eds.) (1995) *Constructivism in Psychotherapy*. Washington, DC: American Psychological Association.

Neimeyer, R. (1998) *Lessons of Loss: A Guide to Coping*. New York, NY: McGraw-Hill.

Orwell, G. (1933) *Down and Out in Paris and London*. London: Victor Gollancz.

Orwell, G. (1936) *The Road to Wigan Pier*. London: Victor Gollancz.

Pennebaker, J.W. and Chung, C.K. (2011) Expressive writing and its links to mental and physical health. In: Friedman, H.S. (ed.) *The Oxford Handbook of Health Psychology*. New York, NY: Oxford University Press.

Pennebaker, J.W. and Chung, C.K. (2012) Expressive writing: connections to physical and mental health. In: Friedman, H.S. (ed.) *The Oxford Handbook of Health Psychology*. [online] Available through: **https://academic.oup.com/**, pp. 417–437. (Accessed 15 January 2014)

Pennebaker, J.W. (1997) *Opening up: The Healing Power of Expressing Emotions*. New York, NY: Guilford.

Porter, M. (2015) *Grief is the Thing with Feathers*. London: Faber and Faber.

Riley, D. (2012) *Time Lived, Without its Flow*. London: Picador.

Rothenberg, A. (1990) *Creativity and Madness: New Findings and Old Stereotypes*. Baltimore, MD: University Press.

Saunders, G. (2017) *Lincoln in the Bardo*. London: Bloomsbury.

Scruton, R. (2021) *Confessions of a Heretic*. Kendal, Cumbria: Notting Hill Editions Ltd.

Sellers, R. and Hogg, J. (2011) *Little Ern: The Authorised Biography of Ernie Wise*. London: Sidgwick & Jackson.

Sontag, S. (2002) *On Photography*. London: Penguin Classics.

Stroebe, M.S., Hansson, R.O., Stroebe, W. and Schut, H. (eds) (1999) *Handbook of Bereavement Research: Consequences, Coping, and Care*. Washington, DC: American Psychological Association.

Wordsworth, W. (1850). *The Prelude*. London: Edward Moxon

Worden, J.W. (1991) *Grief Counselling and Grief Therapy*. 2nd ed. New York, NY: Springer.

**Journals**

Carson, S. (2012) Your Creative Brain. *Cerebral Cortex* [online], 26(5), pp. 1910–2015. Available at: https://www.schweitzer-online.de/ebook/Carson/Your-Creative-Brain/9780470651421/A2061248/ (Accessed 22 March 2019)

Freud, S. (1908) Creative writers and day-dreaming. *Neue Revue* [online], 1(10), pp. 716–724. Available at: **https://www.evergreen.edu/sites/default/files/alumni/images/Freud_Creative_Writers_Daydreaming.pdf** (Accessed 22 March 2019)

Kaufman, J.C. (2011) The Sylvia Plath effect: mental illness in eminent creative writers. *The Journal of Creative Behaviour* [online], 35(1). Available at: https://onlinelibrary.wiley.com/doi/abs/10.1002/j.2162-6057.2001.tb01220.x (Accessed 22 July 2015)

Kaufman, J.C. (2002) I bask in dreams of suicide: mental illness, poetry, and women. *Review of General Psychology* [online], 6(3). Available at: https://journals.sagepub.com/doi/abs/10.1037/1089-2680.6.3.271 (Accessed 22 July 2015)

McCrae, J. (1915) *In Flanders Fields* London: Punch

Muncey, T. (2005) Doing autoethnography. *International Journal of Qualitative Methods* [online], 4 (1), Article 5. Available at: **http://www.ualberta.ca/~iiqm/backissues/4_1/html/muncey.htm** (Accessed 12 March 2014)

Pennebaker, J.W. and Beall, S.K. (1986) Confronting a traumatic event: toward an understanding of inhibition and disease. *Journal of Abnormal Psychology* [online], pp. 95, 274–281. Available at: **https://pubmed.ncbi.nlm.nih.gov/3745650/** (Accessed 25 February 2016)

Sofka, C.J. (1997) Social support 'internetworks,' caskets for sale, and more: thanatology and the information superhighway. *Death*

*Studies* [online], 6, pp. 553–574. Available at: **https://www.researchgate.net/publication/13117946_Social_su pport_Internetworks_caskets_for_sale_and_more_Thanatolo gy_and_the_information_superhighway** (Accessed 15 January 2014)

Stroebe, M. and Schut, H. (1999) The dual process model of coping with bereavement: rationale and description. *Death Studies* [online], 23, pp. 197–224. Available at: **https://pubmed.ncbi.nlm.nih.gov/10848151/** (Accessed 11 January 2016)

Poe, E.A. (1850) The Poetic Principle (reprint). *Home Journal* [online], series for 1850, no. 36 (38), August 31, 1850. Available at: **https://www.eapoe.org/works/essays/poetprnb.htm** (Accessed 19 March 2018)

Walter, T. (1996) A new model of grief: bereavement and biography. *Mortality* [online], 1, pp. 7–25. Available at: **https://www.researchgate.net/publication/240532074_A_New _Model_of_Grief_Bereavement_and_Biography** (Accessed 11 January 2014)

## Websites

Alyssa (2013) *Psychology classics: James Pennebaker's expressive writing paradigm.* [online] Available at: **https://www.psychologyinaction.org/psychology-in-action-1/2013/01/11/classic-psychology-experiments-james-pennebakers-expressive-writing-paradigm** (Accessed 18 May 2019)

BBC.co.uk (2016) *Can exercise really have the same effect as taking illegal drugs?* [online video] Available at: **https://www.bbc.co.uk/bbcthree/article/3259e81b-dc89-477e-ad80-793b06972b16** (Accessed 22 March 2019)

Bryant, R. (2018) *Grief as a psychiatry disorder.* [online] Available at: **https://www.cambridge.org/core/journals/the-british-journal-of-psychiatry/article/grief-as-a-psychiatric-disorder/CE806759C638D2618A2C5BCD122ADDBC** (Accessed 10 May 2018)

Dicks, S. (2017) *The development of a narrative describing the bereavement of families of potential organ donors: a systematic review.* [online] Available at: **https://www.ncbi.nlm.nih.gov/pmc/articles/PMC5779939/** (Accessed 26 November 2018)

Elisabeth Kübler Ross Foundation (2017) *Dr. Elisabeth Kübler-Ross on Oprah Winfrey Show – last appearance 1997.* [online video] Available at: **https://www.youtube.com/watch?v=0kR8VianhSk** (Accessed 9 June 2019)

Eminem (2010) *Difficult (Proof Tribute).* [online] Available at: **https://genius.com/Eminem-difficult-lyrics** (Accessed 2 May 2020)

History (2009) *Hip hop is born at a birthday party in the Bronx.* [online] Available at: **https://www.history.com/this-day-in-history/hip-hop-is-born-at-a-birthday-party-in-the-bronx** (Accessed 29 November 2018)

Hughes, V. (2011) *Shades of grief: when does mourning become a mental illness?* [online] Available at: **https://www.scientificamerican.com/article/shades-of-grief/** (Accessed 13 November 2017)

IMDB (no date) *Eminem Biography.* [online] Available at: **https://www.imdb.com/name/nm0004896/bio** (Accessed 27 November 2018)

Jaden, D. (2013) *Writing effective grief in fiction.* [online] Available at: **http://www.writersdigest.com/editor-blogs/guide-to-literary-agents/writing-effective-grief-in-fiction-5-ideas-for-writers** (Accessed 11 September 2017)

James, J. (2009) *The grief recovery method.* [online] Available at: www.griefrecoverymethod.com (Accessed 22 March 2019)

Kaufman, J. (2001) *The Sylvia Plath effect: mental illness in eminent creative writers.* [online] Available at: **https://www.researchgate.net/publication/260745014_The_S ylvia_Plath_Effect_Mental_Illness_in_Eminent_Creative_ Writers** (Accessed 15 June 2018)

Mantel, H. (2014) *Re-reading CS Lewis: a grief observed.* [online] Available at: **https://www.theguardian.com/books/2014/dec/27/hilary-mantel-rereading-cs-lewis-a-grief-observed** (Accessed 11 May 2014)

McCann, K. (2015) *5 writers who suffered from mental illnesses & the impact it had on their art.* [online] Available at:

http://airshipdaily.com/blog/022620145-writers-mental-illness (Accessed 26 January 2018)

National Health Service (no date) *Overview – Post-traumatic stress disorder.* [online] Available at: https://www.nhs.uk/mental-health/conditions/post-traumatic-stress-disorder-ptsd/overview/ (Accessed 22 March 2019)

Neimeyer, R.A. et al. (2009) *Grief therapy and the reconstruction of meaning: from principles to practice.* [online] Available at: http://hospicewhispers.com/wp-content/uploads/2016/11/NiemeyerGriefTheory.pdf (Accessed 15 January 2014)

Nowinski, J. (2012) *Should grief be a mental illness?* [online] Available at: https://www.psychologytoday.com/gb/blog/the-new-grief/201201/should-grief-be-mental-illness (Accessed 9 March 2017)

Office of National Statistics (2018) *Deaths registered in England and Wales (series DR): 2017.* [online] Available at: https://www.ons.gov.uk/peoplepopulationandcommunity/birthsdeathsandmarriages/deaths/bulletins/deathsregisteredinenglandandwalesseriesdr/2017 (Accessed 11 June 2019)

Park, C. (2014) *Meaning, spirituality and health: a brief introduction.* [online] Available at: https://www.researchgate.net/profile/Crystal_Park/publication/272955903_Meaning_spirituality_and_health_a_brief_introduction/links/ (Accessed 26 November 2018)

Psychology In Action (2013) *Classic psychology experiments.* [online] Available at: https://www.psychologyinaction.org/psychology-in-action-

1/2013/01/11/classic-psychology-experiments-james-pennebakers-expressive-writing-paradigm (Accessed 22 March 2019)

Psychology Today (no date) *Albert Rothenberg – about.* [online] Available at: https://www.psychologytoday.com/intl/experts/albert-rothenberg-md (Accessed 11 June 2018)

Robinson, K.M. (2017) *How writing in a journal helps manage depression.* [online] Available at: https://www.webmd.com/depression/features/writing-your-way-out-of-depression#1 (Accessed 26 November 2018)

Ramis, H. (1994) Groundhog Day.

Rothenberg, A. (2006) *Creativity – the healthy muse.* [online] Available at: https://www.thelancet.com/journals/lancet/article/PIIS0140-6736(06)69905-4/fulltext (Accessed 22 October 2018)

Rothenberg, A. (2015) *Creativity and mental illness.* [online] Available at: https://www.psychologytoday.com/gb/blog/creative-explorations/201503/creativity-and-mental-illness (Accessed 23 September 2017)

Rothenberg, A. (2015) *Creativity and mental illness II: the scream.* [online] Available at: https://www.psychologytoday.com/gb/blog/creative-explorations/201503/creativity-and-mental-illness-ii-the-scream (Accessed 15 June 2018)

Silverman, P.R. (2012) *Raising grieving children*. [online] Available at: **https://www.psychologytoday.com/gb/blog/raising-grieving-children/201202/grief-can-last-lifetime** (Accessed 22 March 2019)

Smith Bailey, D. (2003) *The Sylvia Plath effect*. [online] Available at: **http://www.apa.org/monitor/nov03/plath.aspx** (Accessed 5 May 2018)

Turner, W. (2017) *Reflections on C S Lewis' A Grief Observed*. [online] Available at: **http://www.weldonturner.com/reflections-on-c-s-lewis-a-grief-observed/** (Accessed 15 June 2017)

Welcher, E. (2014) *5 lessons from C S Lewis' Grief Observed*. [online] Available at: **http://gcdiscipleship.com/2014/09/14/5-lessons-from-c-s-lewis-grief-observed/** (Accessed 28 January 2016)

West, J. (2012) How Hollywood reinvented CS Lewis in the film Shadowlands. [online] Available at **https://cslewisweb.com/2012/07/02/how-hollywood-reinvented-c-s-lewis-in-the-film-shadowlands/** (Accessed 24 May 2021)

Wright, K. (2021) *'Pouring one out' explained: history, meaning & getting it right*. [online] Available at: https://www.joincake.com/blog/pour-one-out/ (Accessed 26 April 2021

*All references are in line with the Harvard Reference guide issued by LJMU (2015)*